Bowing and curtsying were originally signs of being humble; the person with the least authority bows lowest. Bowing is a mark of respect common to most cultures. In Japan bowing is a complicated business, especially if it is unclear who is superior, or if no one wants to give up their importance. Whoever is junior must keep bowing until the superior one straightens up.

German men used to click their heels together when bowing, as if they were soldiers standing to attention. This became fashionable in the nineteenth century when Germany was a militaristic society.

Some Indians greet each other by pressing their hands together, as if in prayer. They say 'Namaste' while bowing slightly. This is a special mark of respect and is a way of greeting the god within the person.

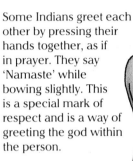

In many Eastern countries it is considered impolite to approach people directly. Where the weather is hot there may be no doors on the houses. Instead of knocking, a visitor may stand outside and cough quietly.

When Alphonso XIII, King of Spain, visited Italy in 1923, the populace greeted him by rattling keys to ward off his evil influence. Earlier in his visit to Italy his sailors had suffered fatal accidents and a dam had collapsed at Lake Gleno as his train passed by. ►

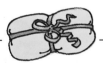

Oh, you shouldn't have!

Giving flowers can be a risky business. Roses usually signify romantic intentions; yellow flowers in Bulgaria mean hatred; carnations are traditionally used in funeral wreaths in Norway.

In Turkey and the Far East, opening a gift when it is presented is thought impolite. This is because it distracts the host's attention from the guest. In Europe and the United States gifts are opened immediately, because to wait might be thought ungrateful.

If you bring a bottle of wine to a dinner in France, you may not get to drink it. Your host should have carefully selected the wine to match the food prepared.

Don't bring a bottle of wine to dinner in Spain, Portugal or Italy. Your host may think that you are questioning his or her ability to provide a decent bottle.

TALKING AND WRITING

Once the greetings are out of the way, people can start to talk to each other. But even in conversation we obey certain ancient rules and customs. Some of these are instinctive, but others are learnt as a part of our culture.

In some cultures people stand close together when they talk, often touching each other. In other cultures, such as in northern Europe, they stand far apart. People from southern cultures may think this looks unfriendly.

Body language

You can tell whom people are most interested in within a group of people by looking at everybody's feet. The feet tend to point towards that person. People also lean towards an interesting speaker.

The art of talking

The art of talking is taking turns. If everybody speaks at once, no one is understood. In Western cultures it is polite for the listener to glance at the person talking. When their eyes meet he or she will have an opportunity to take over. The person talking may look away to avoid losing control of the conversation.

The right way to write?

Writing is a bit like speaking and there's no agreement on how it should be done.

The ancient Greeks wrote from left to right, then on the next line from right to left. This method is presumably quicker than writing in just one direction.

Arabic is written from right to left.

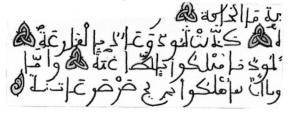

```
ΛEIϹIΛTIOIϹϹIMϢΛ
IIϹIΓOϹYIIΛIϢΛN
ΛIϹYϹIN·ΛϹIOYϹIN
ΛYIϢΊϹΡΧΟΜϹΟΛΚ
IIMϹIϹϹYNϹΚINIII
OONOYNΚΛIϹNϹI
```

The Chinese and Japanese write from the top to the bottom of the page.

In the West writing goes from left to right. This probably developed because it was easier for right-handed people to write this way with a pen, without smudging the ink.

Writing backwards?
If you are left-handed, you may find it more natural to write from right to left like Leonardo da Vinci used to. Other people would have to read your writing by reflecting it in a mirror.

4

Formal talking

Some conversations get very heated. Debates about important issues are especially likely to overheat, and most cultures have developed special customs to prevent people shouting in formal debates.

Native American men share a peace pipe when debating difficult issues.

Some African peoples take turns to discuss things by passing around a stick. Only the person holding the stick is allowed to talk.

In the British House of Commons, the opposing seats are positioned two sword lengths away from each other. Members must address their opponents politely as the Honourable or Right Honourable Member, even when they are not feeling friendly. This is thought to make it more difficult for them to insult each other.

In some formal meetings, speakers must always speak to the chairperson, or 'chair', and not to anyone else. This helps to keep things calm as opponents can't address each other directly.

But is it true?

When people tell lies, they tend to avoid eye-contact, and the palms of their hands may get hot. Machines called lie detectors can be used to help decide if somebody is telling the truth or not. They work by measuring body changes, for example, an increase in sweat.

When telling lies some people cross their fingers. The cross is a sign of protection in Christian cultures – the people who cross their fingers are protecting themselves from the Devil, sometimes called the Father of Lies.

COURTING

In all societies there are rules about who can marry whom, and about how people should behave towards the opposite sex. These rules vary from those of Islamic countries, where women are instructed to keep themselves covered in front of men who are not their close relations, to traditions about dating in North America.

The kiss may have evolved from mothers chewing and passing on food to their children. When lovers kiss, they re-enact this caring role with each other.

The Sambia men of New Guinea fear that the women may take their strength away. Women can only walk along certain 'women's paths'. They are forbidden to touch men's heads, weapons, and ritual ornaments.

In rural Africa brides may be bought in exchange for cattle. The price is negotiated between families. In India, on the other hand, the bride's family had to give a dowry to the bridegroom and his family. Women were sometimes married just for their dowries. The dowry system is now illegal in India.

St Valentine's day dates back to the Roman feast of Lupercalia, which was held on February 15. Over the years, a custom evolved where unmarried men were required to pick a girl's name from a lottery and court her for the rest of the year. Later the lottery ticket was accompanied by a card and a gift.

Traditionally, Chinese people of the opposite sex do not touch each other in public, though it is quite common to see men walking along hand-in-hand. Kissing in public is considered very bad manners.

In the West, men are traditionally expected to let women walk through doorways first. In the East it's the other way round. However, nowadays, some women feel insulted if doors are opened for them – they feel this gesture takes away their independence.

Women wearing long dresses needed help to climb into a horse-drawn carriage. Some women still expect car doors to be held open for them.

In the West, men traditionally walk between women and the road. This arrangement allowed men to protect women from mudsplashes caused by passing carriages. Women still had to take care, however, since in the past, people used to empty their chamberpots out of windows!

Chaperones

Royal or noble European girls used to be accompanied by female chaperones to make sure that the girls did not talk to unsuitable men. There were ways, though, to avoid the chaperone's control. If the girl saw a man she liked, she would drop her umbrella to attract his eye; dropping the umbrella twice meant 'I love you'.

▲ Weddings

In many Western countries, wedding rings are worn on the third finger of the left hand. It was believed that a nerve ran up the finger straight to the heart, the seat of love and faithfulness.

Rice was used as confetti because it was a symbol of fertility. In Roman times, nuts, sweets, or pieces of wheat were used.

The ancient Teutons of northern Europe used to drink mead, a honey wine, for a month after their wedding. This month was known as the honeymoon. At that time it was the custom for a man to kidnap his intended bride and hide her from her family until she agreed to marry him. The couple would then come out of hiding. To this day, the destination of honeymooners should be secret.

IN THE STREET

All cultures have rules about how to behave in public places. What is considered normal behaviour in one country may be very rude in another. One of the first lessons to learn when going abroad is how not to offend the locals.

In Tokyo special pushers are employed to push people onto crowded trains during the rush hour, so that as many people as possible can get on.

In Saudi Arabia women go to the front of queues in public buildings so that they don't have to remain too long in public near strange men.

In Japan it is rude to blow your nose in public.

Spitting

Spitting was once very common, particularly when the habit of chewing tobacco was widespread.

In India, people spit after chewing on betel nuts. Sikhs and Hindus must ritually clean their throats each morning, which often makes a lot of noise.

Traditions about driving on the left or right date back to the days when people rode horses. It was easier for swordsmen to mount from the left, so that their swords did not get in the way. Mounting-blocks were therefore sited on the left side of the road. Also it was safer to pass strangers on the left, so that, if necessary, a sword could be wielded with the right hand.

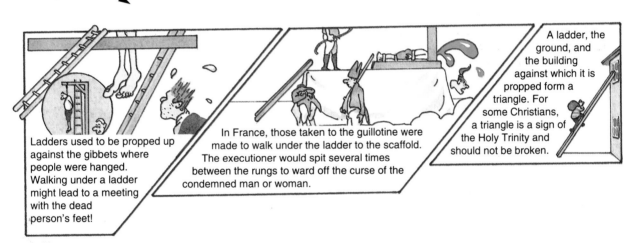

Unlucky ladders

Ladders used to be propped up against the gibbets where people were hanged. Walking under a ladder might lead to a meeting with the dead person's feet!

In France, those taken to the guillotine were made to walk under the ladder to the scaffold. The executioner would spit several times between the rungs to ward off the curse of the condemned man or woman.

A ladder, the ground, and the building against which it is propped form a triangle. For some Christians, a triangle is a sign of the Holy Trinity and should not be broken.

Litter

In much of Germany, householders are responsible for sweeping up litter from the pavement in front of their houses, so that the streets are kept clean.

In most cultures dropping litter is frowned upon or illegal. Singapore is especially clean; chewing gum is illegal because of the mess it can cause on the streets.

GRUB'S UP!

Eating together is a sign of friendship. The host gives food and drink to the guest and the guest shows appreciation. All societies have special customs for eating, and it is insulting to those eating with you to ignore their customs.

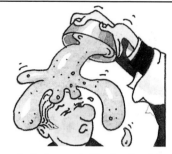

In India people hiss to attract the attention of waiters. Don't try this in the West – if you want your meal served at all!

Bad manners

Sitting with your elbows on the table is considered bad manners – the form of your posture excludes those on either side of you.

Smoking is now considered not only rude to non-smokers, but very unhealthy for everybody.

In all cultures farting is considered a sign of bad manners, for obvious reasons...

Eating with your mouth open is bad manners because people can see the food churning around in your mouth, which is not a pretty sight. However, in parts of Africa it is polite to make a noise by smacking your lips while eating.

Being sick at the table is disapproved of in most cultures.

Good manners ▲

Africa and the East

In parts of Africa it is polite to belch.

In the Far East it is polite to pass food with two hands.

In New Guinea, people must share food with whoever is around at the time of the meal. If they haven't enough food, then whatever food there is must be hidden, and no one may eat until the guests have left.

In some cultures, to surprise your hosts by turning up early is as bad as not coming at all. In Japan it is customary to arrive one hour late, and in Greece, half an hour late.

Hospitality in the desert

It is said that a certain Bedu sheik, on hearing a wolf howl, would tell his son to send a goat into the desert. The sheik believed that nothing should go hungry while near him – except possibly the goat!

Guests of desert Arabs are treated with great hospitality. Tradition holds that an uninvited guest can stay for three days and is to be defended against all attacks.

Before news is discussed between travellers, coffee is drunk as a sign of hospitality. No bad news, not even disasters, may be related before one or two cups of coffee have been taken.

In the Middle East, guests should not study their food because that would seem greedy. Instead they should pay attention to their host. Some Arabs say it is impossible to make an enemy of someone who has shared salt with you.

Salt

Salt is important in many cultures because of its use in food preparation. A certain amount of salt is also necessary for health.

In India, soldiers express loyalty to their employer saying that they have 'taken his salt'.

Among the Ibo of Nigeria, children eat with their mothers. The father sits some way away as a sign of prestige. If he has many wives, the man must accept a piece of food from each of them: to refuse any wife would be a sign that he suspected her of poisoning him.

Eating other people is strongly disapproved of all over the world, even if the person is already dead. In the past cannibalism was widely practised. Human flesh is said to taste like pork. In fact, Melanesians of the South Pacific used to refer to human flesh as 'long pig'.

If a guest failed to turn up to a party in nineteenth-century Paris, a professional guest could be hired to take his place.

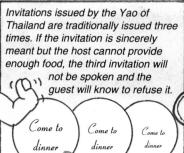

Invitations issued by the Yao of Thailand are traditionally issued three times. If the invitation is sincerely meant but the host cannot provide enough food, the third invitation will not be spoken and the guest will know to refuse it.

Come to dinner
Come to dinner
Come to dinner

In the ancient Middle East, the host would pour perfumed oil over the heads of the guests. This was to mark their passage from the 'dirty' outside to the 'pure' interior.

ACTING POSH

Big feasts can be a way to show off power and riches. The order in which people are seated at table shows who is most important, while the richness and quantity of food, drink and tableware shows the wealth of the host. Big feasts are often very formal.

Romans liked to invite odd numbers of guests, since to them even numbers meant conflict. Nowadays in Western countries an even number of men and women is usually preferred, to help the flow of conversation.

Posh manners and the use of lots of cutlery were encouraged by women when the sexes began to feast together frequently from the sixteenth and seventeenth centuries onwards. Women disliked the boorish, drunken behaviour of the men. Until recently they left the table before the men, so that the men could carry on drinking.

It was once traditional for a male guest to be given an envelope containing the name of the lady he was to accompany to the table. The couple would then walk to the dinner table together.

When sitting down to a place at a table surrounded by many knives, forks and spoons, the rule is to start at the outside and work inwards.

Food is served from the left to avoid knocking over wine glasses, which are placed on the right. Wine is served from the right to avoid leaning over the diner.

Originally, dish covers were not used to keep the food warm but to stop others popping poison onto the dish.

Head-wear at dinner

In ancient Greece and Rome, guests at a banquet wore wreaths of plaited flowers and leaves. They believed these would prevent drunkenness.

The ancient Egyptians wore cones of perfumed wax on their heads. The wax melted during the evening and ran down their faces in a stream, cooling the diners.

To drink to someone is to wish that person good health. This has been done since very ancient times.

In early northern Europe, feasts were male affairs and the men got very drunk. Among the ancient Celts the thighbones of a bird were reserved for the most important guests. Men would fight to the death over thighbones.

Smashing wine glasses after a toast is said to show that the friendship toasted can never be un-toasted. The Greeks traditionally break large quantities of plates after big dinners.

KINGS AND QUEENS

Kings and queens expect to be treated differently from other people. In fact, special treatment is part of the way they enforce their power. Take the case of Kao-tsu, a Chinese peasant who rose to power in ancient China and founded the Han dynasty. He disliked all the ceremony of the royal court, so he abolished most of the court rituals. This caused his followers to stop respecting him. They drunkenly disrupted court audiences and vandalized his palace. Kao-tsu made new rules to replace the ones he had abolished: he was to be borne into the palace on a litter, heralded by hundreds of banner-waving courtiers. Soon everyone treated him as an emperor again.

Meeting royalty

Women are expected to curtsy. Men are expected to bow.

Shake hands if a hand is offered.

It is bad manners to meet royalty with gloves on since, in the past, gloves were associated with gauntlets and warfare.

Until recently it was thought impolite to turn one's back on the King or Queen of England. People would walk backwards out of their presence. In certain ceremonies lords and other officials still do.

Footmen are still employed by Western royalty. These days they do little more than stand silently by the door. Their original role may have been to check visitors for weapons.

It is considered offensive to offer a weapon as a gift. As recently as 1979, when opening a public building, the Queen of the United Kingdom refused to accept the scissors offered. Instead, she used an old sixpenny piece to cut the ribbon.

Why! That's odd!

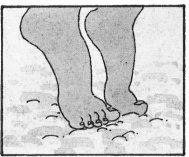

The traditional 'Moundang', or ruler, in Chad, in North Africa, was so powerful that no one could watch him eating, for fear of disturbing his sacred force. His greatness was such that he was followed by a slave, who collected his excreta.

The Kabaka of Uganda at his court in Kampala always walked on tiptoe to demonstrate his superiority to his subjects.

The great fourteenth-century Moroccan traveller, Ibn Battuta, described the court of the Mansa of the Malian Empire in northwest Africa. The Mansa would execute anyone who sneezed or wore sandals in his presence. Whenever he spoke his courtiers would murmur approval.

All people were obliged to prostrate themselves on the floor, or kowtow in submission before the Emperor of China. The first British ambassador to the Chinese court refused to do this because it would have meant that the British Empire was inferior to the Chinese Empire. The Chinese avoided the problem by saying that the ambassador was a barbarian who did not understand good manners, and he was eventually allowed to meet the Emperor standing up.

At royal feasts, in seventeenth-century Europe, food would be sculpted by artists who would spend days preparing it. Spectators would watch the nobility feasting, and when they finished, the spectators would rush to the tables and eat some of the leftovers.

King Louis XIV of France made everything he did into a ceremony in order to keep his nobles occupied. High nobles fought for the privilege of doing tasks such as carrying the royal slippers. The king would get up twice each morning – once in private, and once in a 'levee' when crowds of courtiers would watch him.

In the West, we stand to show respect when someone important enters the room. But in the Middle East it is rude to stand higher than your host, and so one remains seated until given permission to stand.

SCHOOL AND WORK

All over the world, adults spend their lives working, and in most countries children either work or go to school. It has been estimated, though, that the San pygmies of Southern Africa only need to work for two or three days a week to support themselves. This is because, although the Kalahari desert is not very productive, the people are very skilled hunters and gatherers. Modern civilization has brought many comforts, but people have to work harder to get them. The San, on the other hand, have fewer luxuries but work less.

Many countries have long summer holidays. Summer is harvest time and the time of year when, in the past, children were most needed to help on the farm. Hot countries have long summer holidays because it is too hot to sit and study in school.

Weekends off are a recent thing. Christians used to work every day except Sunday, but had holidays on several days scattered through the year. As more and more people started to work in factories, in the eighteenth and nineteenth centuries, regular holidays became a necessity.

In parts of Africa, markets take place every five days. In the past, Africans used a five-day week, and the markets still follow this system.

Different religions have different Sabbaths, or days of rest. Christians don't work on Sundays, Muslims on Fridays and Jews on Saturdays.

In some Far Eastern cultures, such as that of Korea, great respect is shown to authority. Pupils stand up and bow when the teacher enters the classroom, and workers stand up and bow when a senior manager enters the office. The culture is based on the writings of the ancient Chinese philosopher Confucius, who emphasized the need to respect older people and authority. In the Far East it is thought rude for pupils to question their teachers.

Separate sexes

In Saudi Arabia, business meetings between men and women must be conducted from different rooms over an intercom system. Businesswomen must not drive cars and can only be driven from place to place by close male relatives.

Business cards

In Japan you should offer your business card with two hands. In order to show respect you should carefully study any card which you are given before a meeting. Then you should place it, face upwards, on the table in front of you, and leave it there during the meeting.

Teachers in the Pacific Islands avoid praising their pupils. Schoolchildren feel ashamed if they are praised or if they are criticized in front of their friends. ►

In Japan, companies are seen as extended families, and many Japanese see more of their bosses and co-workers than they do of their real families. If they are too old or unable to work profitably for their company, Japanese workers may be placed by the windows of their offices so that they can look out. They are known as 'window-men'. ◄

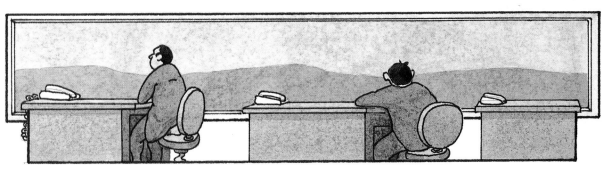

AT HOME

Travellers away from home need a safe haven, and in the past this would often be someone's house. Most cultures have a tradition of honouring guests, but guests are also dangerous because they enter our homes yet are not part of the family. There are unwritten rules about how guests and hosts should behave towards each other.

When the Irish enter a house, they traditionally say 'God bless all here except the cat' because the cat was once considered an evil creature. Medieval Europeans thought cats were agents of the Devil.

In ancient Greece, men who entertained each other in their homes would create a friendship bond that lasted for generations. Descendants of friends, meeting for the first time on the battle-field, would not fight each other.

When visiting someone in the Far East, it is polite to remove one's shoes so that the dirt from outside is not brought into the house.

In many cultures people do not sit on chairs, but recline on divans or sit on cushions on the floor. When sitting like this in the Middle East, it is impolite to point the sole of the shoe towards people, since it has come into contact with the dirty ground.

Inuits are hospitable people, even though the far north where they live may not seem to be very welcoming. Traditionally, a man might offer his wife to sleep with a guest as a gesture of hospitality, and also as a means of securing lifelong friendship and aid.

On entering a house men should remove their hats and put down their sticks. This comes from the custom of removing a helmet and sword as a gesture of peace.

18

People in different cultures have various ways of living together.

The Chinese like to have several generations of the family living together.

Some South Asian tribespeople live communally in 'long-houses'.

Modern communes consist of groups of people, not all belonging to the same family, who share living accommodation and property.

Polygyny, common in parts of Africa and Asia, is when one man is married to more than one woman.

Polyandry, which occurs in parts of India, is when one woman is married to more than one man.

In some families in Arabia the women and children live in the harem, or women's quarters. Adult male guests can only enter a room called the majlis. This is because of the segregation of the sexes required by the culture.

The nuclear family is common in the West. It consists of a mother, a father and their children. These days, however, many children in the West live with only one of their parents.

Among many early peoples of Europe and Asia the horse was sacred. Today, lucky horseshoes are normally nailed open-side up, so that the luck doesn't drain out of them. However, they may be nailed the other way round to prevent evil spirits from entering the house from the underworld.

In the West, gargoyles are used to ward off evil. They are made as ugly as possible to scare off evil spirits. ◄

Early umbrellas from the Far East were very unreliable and could open suddenly. It was safest not to open them indoors. Doing this came to be thought of as unlucky.

At the time of Christ, shaking the dust off one's feet on leaving was a sign of disapproval.

In some African countries, when a man leaves one tribe to live with a new tribe, he brings a handful of earth from his old home, mixes it with water and some soil from his new home, and drinks the resulting concoction. This symbolizes that he is combining the spirit of his old homeland with that of the new.

19

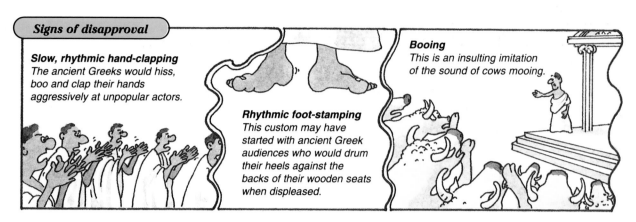

Slow, rhythmic hand-clapping
The ancient Greeks would hiss, boo and clap their hands aggressively at unpopular actors.

Rhythmic foot-stamping
This custom may have started with ancient Greek audiences who would drum their heels against the backs of their wooden seats when displeased.

Booing
This is an insulting imitation of the sound of cows mooing.

ENTERTAINMENT

It takes a lot of courage to stand up on stage in front of a crowd of people. Staring eyes are a sign of aggression, and thousands of staring eyes can be very frightening. Audiences have many ways of showing their approval or disapproval. These are remarkably similar all over the world. Performers are frequently sick with fear when struck with stage-fright, and many actors have died of heart attacks on stage.

Modern theatres have their origin in ancient Greece, when masked actors would put on plays in specially-built theatres. The plays would often comment on the political situation.

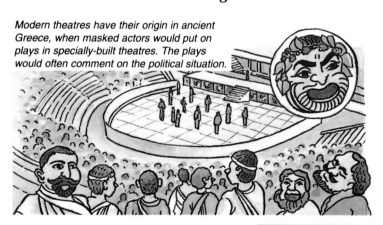

If an execution was part of the plot in a Roman play, a real criminal was sometimes executed on stage.

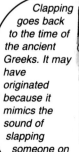

Clapping goes back to the time of the ancient Greeks. It may have originated because it mimics the sound of slapping someone on the back, which shows approval.

In China the performers clap as well as the audience.

The ancient Romans snapped their fingers and, if they were really pleased, waved the pointed ends of their togas.

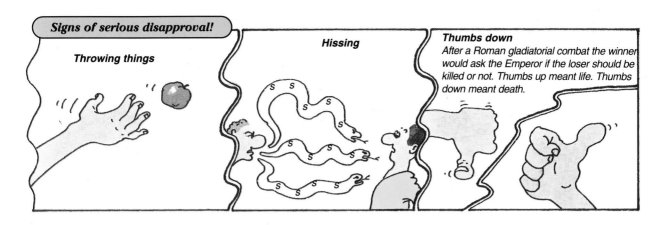

Throwing things

Hissing

Thumbs down
After a Roman gladiatorial combat the winner would ask the Emperor if the loser should be killed or not. Thumbs up meant life. Thumbs down meant death.

Parasites were early entertainers. They were poor Romans, invited as second-class guests to the banquets of the rich. Sometimes they shared the food, sometimes they were given cheaper food. They were made fun of by the proper guests and had to sit on stools instead of reclining on couches.

Medieval jesters were used for entertainment in the same way as parasites. They originated as guests with special peculiarities which made people laugh. Henry II's jester, Roland, was granted a job for himself and his heirs in return for a 'leap, a whistle and a fart'.

More signs of approval

Flowers are given to leading actresses, singers and dancers.

Money and flowers may be thrown on stage.

Audiences clap enthusiastically and shout 'Encore' when they want musicians to carry on playing.

In the seventeenth century, whistling, stamping and clapping accompanied church services until ministers forbade it.

In the Middle East money is tucked into the belts of belly dancers.

At the end of a performance, the actors bow and the curtain closes. If the audience continues to clap the curtains reopen and the performers bow again. This may happen several times.

In the past, men practised sports during peacetime to keep themselves fit for fighting. Sport has also provided entertainment. The game of football has been popular for more than two thousand years. The first recorded game was played in China around 400 BC. The game was illegal in England from 1314 for almost two hundred years, although no one took much notice of the law. In the sixteenth century Philip Stubbs described the game as causing 'fighting, brawling, contention, quarrel picking, murder and great effusions of blood'.

SPORT

In July 1969, high emotions over a football match led to a war between El Salvador and Honduras which lasted a month. 3,000 people are said to have died.

From the earliest times, there has been a need for a neutral person to have authority over games. Umpires were originally called *noumperes*, meaning non-peer or not-equal, which meant that they had the authority to judge disputes between players.

In June 1817, both the England cricket team and the Nottinghamshire side they were playing were accused of cheating by trying to lose. The England player William Lambert is said to have deliberately dropped catches and some Nottinghamshire players had betted on England winning the match.

Today, competition between athletes is so fierce that some competitors cheat by taking illegal drugs, which help them perform better. To check that the competition is fair, athletes may be tested for drugs in their blood after competing.

Not all sports participants in the past have been men. In the 1720s there was a famous prize-fighter called Elizabeth Stokes.

In the 800 m women's race at the Amsterdam Olympics in 1928, five women collapsed and five dropped out. Only the winner completed the race, and she fainted.

The Olympic games were originally part of an ancient Greek religious festival and were held from 776 BC to AD 393. They were then banned by the Christians. The games were revived in the Cotswold Olympics in 1612, and then in the town of Much Wenlock in England in the nineteenth century. By the 1870s the games had grown into a large athletics meeting at which laurel wreaths were given to the winners. This meeting was visited by the Frenchman, Baron de Coubertin. He had the idea of starting a truly international athletics meeting, to encourage peaceful international competition.

Sports fans are as old as sport itself. In ancient Rome there were four chariot teams: the reds, the blues, the greens and the whites. Fights between supporters were common and sometimes deadly. In AD 532, fighting broke out between rival fans at a sports meeting at the Hippodrome Stadium in Constantinople. Imperial soldiers were sent to quell the riot which developed into an all-out revolt against the Emperor in which 30,000 lives were lost.

The first circus took place in ancient Rome, and was connected to a religious occasion. 'Circus' comes from the Latin word for a ring. In AD 107 the Emperor Trajan staged a contest with five thousand pairs of gladiators, many of whom fought to the death in the ring.

Bull-fighting comes from the ancient art of bull-jumping in Crete. The male and female dancers would get the bull to charge them, then grip its horns and vault over its back.

MAKING PICTURES

Since the origins of humankind, pictures and images, such as Stone Age cave paintings, have been thought to have magical power. Nowadays we are bombarded with images from television, cinema and magazines. Many children watch up to eight hours of television each day.

Images clearly have a powerful attraction. Perhaps the early belief that they had magical power is correct.

It is thought that ceremonies involving painting and singing were held to bring success in hunting. Early cave paintings are often found in parts of caves where the acoustics are particularly good.

People who spend all their time watching television are called 'couch potatoes'. This is probably because they 'plant' themselves on a sofa, and grow fat through lack of exercise and eating too many potato chips.

Throughout the world there are many statues and images of gods or other religious figures. Some believers think that the god actually lives in the statue. Others use the statue as a way of thinking about the god. Ancient Greek statues were originally brightly painted, to look as realistic as possible.

The first soap operas were broadcast on the radio. They were made by US soap manufacturers as a way of advertising their products. Most 'soaps' are now on TV.

In some homes, it is considered polite to switch off the television when a guest arrives, so that people don't have to talk over the sound of the programme.

Devout Muslims believe that pictures of real things are blasphemous. Only God can create real things: pictures are just imitations. This belief has led to the Muslim tradition of creating beautiful geometric patterns.

Photography of women is unwelcome in many Middle Eastern countries, where it is thought that women are not for public display. In Saudi Arabia there are no public cinemas. In Africa some people will not allow their pictures to be taken: they believe that a photograph may capture the subject's soul.

Many paints are highly poisonous. When painters mixed their own pigments they were often poisoned by lead, mercury, cadmium, cobalt or arsenic. The French Impressionist painter, Renoir, may have developed arthritis from metal poisoning. His hands became rigid claws and he could paint only with a brush tied to his arm.

Some people don't like images, especially religious images. Such people are called iconoclasts, after a movement of eighth- and ninth-century Byzantines who disapproved of 'icons' or religious pictures, and smashed them up. The tradition was revived by the puritans in the sixteenth century, some of whom were responsible for breaking up thousands of church carvings all over north-west Europe.

Unlucky mirrors! ▲

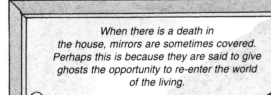

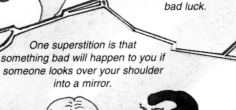

When there is a death in the house, mirrors are sometimes covered. Perhaps this is because they are said to give ghosts the opportunity to re-enter the world of the living.

It is said that breaking a mirror brings seven years' bad luck.

One superstition is that something bad will happen to you if someone looks over your shoulder into a mirror.

Vampires are said to have no reflection. They are supposed to be 'undead' and not part of the real world; thus their images cannot be seen in a mirror. So if you don't see a vampire in a mirror it can be either lucky or very unlucky!

Medieval Italians bit their thumb at an enemy. Sticking out the tongue is still an aggressive gesture.

As a sign of anger, Greeks thrust an open hand in a person's face. In ancient times, criminals were paraded through the streets to be jeered at. People would scoop up handfuls of filth and smear it in the criminals' faces.

People who want to appear bigger and tougher than they are puff out their chests.

FIGHTING

Male gorillas beat their chests as a threatening gesture.

People and animals often settle their differences by fighting. Fights between members of the same species do not normally end in death. This is because neither combatant wants to risk his or her life. Instead the combatants try to look more frightening than the fight itself. People are more likely to end up killing each other than animals are.

Formal fighting techniques

Jousting imitated medieval warfare, but reduced the danger. Combatants charged at each other with lances. It was also practice for proper warfare.

There are as many different styles of wrestling as there are different cultures. Perhaps the oddest is sumo wrestling, where the combatants eat huge amounts of food so that they reach enormous weights.

Boxing was a very bloody sport until modern boxing gloves were introduced in the nineteenth century. 'Bruisers' fought with bare knuckles to the point of exhaustion, unconsciousness or even death. Some ancient Greek boxers even wore metal bars strapped to their fists.

An ancient Greek boxing glove

Duelling did not always end in death. The combatants frequently fought to wound and first blood ended the conflict. Duels were normally fought with pistols or swords. The modern sport of fencing is directly related to duelling with swords.

In the West it is rude to point. The index finger was once thought to be poisonous.

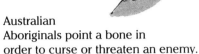

Australian Aboriginals point a bone in order to curse or threaten an enemy.

To challenge someone to a fight in medieval times, one struck the person with a glove, or threw it at his or her feet. If the challenge was accepted the person picked up the glove. To this day one should not thank someone who picks up a dropped glove.

Among the Sambia of New Guinea an ample secretion of sweat, mucus, blood, urine and semen is a sign of strength. Strength is considered important and men are judged by it. After a truce combatants shake hands, exchange cowrie shells and spit ginger at each other's faces and bodies. The ginger is thought to dispel the ghosts of dead warriors. Ghosts are thought to dislike the smell of ginger.

The Celtic queen Boadicea fought the Romans with a hare-skin next to her breast, for luck. The hare was a sacred animal to the Celts. Later the hare was confused with the rabbit and the tradition of a lucky rabbit's foot arose.

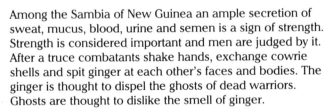

Like most animals, the human victor will stop attacking once the victim shows he or she has given up.

Shaking hands at the end of a fight shows that weapons are no longer being held.

White flags are possibly used for surrender because, in heraldry, white symbolizes innocence and honesty.

Forcing captives to walk under the yolk was a Roman practice that symbolized the submission of prisoners of war.

Holding your hands up. This shows that you are not carrying a weapon.

Kissing the dirt shows that the victim is unworthy to kiss the feet of the victor.

Curling up in a ball is an instinctive reaction. It protects most of the vital organs of the body.

27

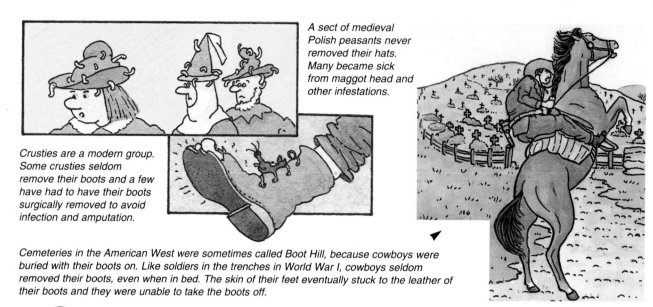

A sect of medieval Polish peasants never removed their hats. Many became sick from maggot head and other infestations.

Crusties are a modern group. Some crusties seldom remove their boots and a few have had to have their boots surgically removed to avoid infection and amputation.

Cemeteries in the American West were sometimes called Boot Hill, because cowboys were buried with their boots on. Like soldiers in the trenches in World War I, cowboys seldom removed their boots, even when in bed. The skin of their feet eventually stuck to the leather of their boots and they were unable to take the boots off.

CLEAN AND NOT SO CLEAN

Bacteria in dirt can cause illness. It is necessary to be clean in order to be healthy, although too much washing can damage the skin and destroy the body's natural defensive bacteria. Because of the importance for health of washing, it has acquired a special significance in many cultures. From ancient times people have believed that water cleans the spirit as well as the body. Christian baptism is a ritual cleansing. Devout Hindus wash in the Ganges at least once in their lifetimes, and Muslims must wash before prayers.

Catholics make the sign of the cross on themselves with holy water. This is double protection because both the sign of the cross and the water are barriers against evil.

Washing once caused a war! When twentieth-century missionaries in New Guinea taught the Wunyu-Sambia to wash, their neighbours, the Seboolu people, thought the Wunyu-Sambia were imitating their purification ritual. The Wunyu-Sambia also boasted that their washing made them 'more manly' than the Seboolu. Angry at this 'theft of customs', the Seboolu attacked the Wunyu-Sambia.

Nowadays people swim in the sea for pleasure, but at one time sea water was thought to be dangerous. In the eighteenth century, the idea that immersion in sea-water was healthy gained ground. First it was drunk. Then bathing started, although strictly for health. This caused the rise of coastal resorts and leisure swimming.

Baths without water

The Nuer of southern Sudan wash their hands and faces in the urine of cattle. They cover their bodies, dress their hair and clean their teeth in the ashes of cow dung.

According to medieval superstition, virgins should bathe in milk to keep their youth and beauty.

Nowadays we brush our hair to get rid of tangles and to make it look good. Before shampoos were invented, people would brush their hair for health. They would brush repeatedly to remove dust and to spread the oils from the glands in the roots through to the rest of the hair.

Saunas are especially popular in the cold countries of northern Europe. People steam themselves until they are very hot, then run outside, roll in the snow and beat each other with birch twigs. This makes them feel warm and glowing.

Guests in Japan usually bathe as soon as they arrive at the guest house. The Japanese first wash and rinse off entirely before entering the bath. This is because other guests will be using the same water.

In the Middle Ages, it was said that a witch could be identified by her reaction to running water. It was thought she would recoil from its purity. Running water tends to be much cleaner than still water, because micro-organisms cannot grow in it so easily.

29

SAYING GOODBYE

In some cultures saying goodbye is an elaborate ritual which involves shaking hands and embracing even with quite distant acquaintances. Other cultures encourage more restrained behaviour. It can even be considered bad luck to turn round and look back. For instance, in the Bible, Lot's wife turned round for a last look at the city of Sodom, and was turned into a pillar of salt.

Saying goodbye can be difficult. People often put it off as long as possible, and so soften the parting. Many of the expressions in different languages for goodbye mean 'See you soon'. The closeness of the relationship between people is shown by how far they walk from the house when they have to part. If the relationship is a close one, people will walk to the end of the driveway or even the street. This delays the moment of parting.

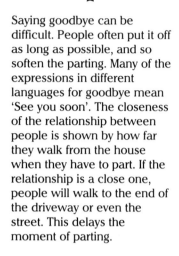

We wave goodbye to people we wish to see again soon. One reason suggested for the custom of waving is that it echoes the action of beckoning someone back.

In Japan, departing guests are given presents which are carefully wrapped in several layers.

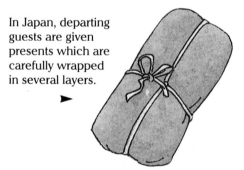

Sailors' wives, saying goodbye before a long trip, might throw their left shoes after the ship to wish their loved ones a safe voyage.

Death is the final parting, and all cultures have invented elaborate rituals for expressing grief and for conducting funerals. In some cultures, women make a special crying noise when someone dies. It is a high-pitched and dramatic noise. This is called ululating or keening.

Just about everything people do has been thought to bring bad luck or be bad mannered at some time, or in some place. Can you spot the rude, or unlucky, things Nora does on this page? There is at least one thing in each picture.

NAUGHTY NORA'S

ANSWERS:

1: Painting pictures (p25). **2:** Kissing in public (p6), standing close to each other (p17), looking over Mum's shoulder into rear-view mirror (p25). **3:** Nora gets Mum to drive (p4). **4:** Rushing straight into Palace (p25), not being politely late, or early! **5:** Not standing up for the Queen (p15), showing sole of shoe to Queen (p18), sticking out tongue (p26). **6:** Nora giving gift of yellow flowers (p3), not taking off shoes (p18), shaking hands with gloves on (p14), shaking hands with her left hand (p2). **7:** Nora looking at food closely (p11), when presented to Queen (p12). **8:** Elbows on table (p10), belching (p10), mouth open (p10), using wrong cutlery (p14). **9:** Being photographed outside with award (p25), standing with her back to the Queen (p14). (Note: You may find even more things if you look closely!)

31

WHY DO WE WEAR THAT?

WHO NEEDS CLOTHES?

Why do we wear clothes? After all, for many thousands of years, men and women lived in warm climates without clothes at all. So why did we suddenly decide to get dressed? People wear clothes for lots of reasons.

The way people dress can show which group or country they belong to.

| Cowboy | Rock musician | Peruvian | Farmer | Businesswoman |

There are practical reasons too...

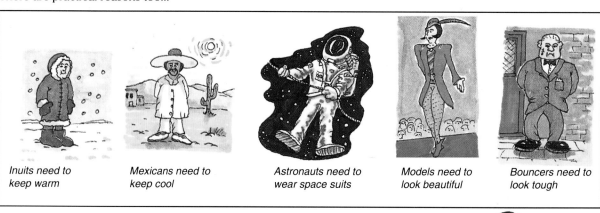

Inuits need to keep warm

Mexicans need to keep cool

Astronauts need to wear space suits

Models need to look beautiful

Bouncers need to look tough

Men and women have tended to dress differently, mainly because people expected them to. These days, however, we feel the differences are not so important. Sometimes men wear women's clothes, and sometimes women wear men's. There are also unisex styles.

Unisex safari suits, 1968

Revival of late eighteenth-century menswear, 1966

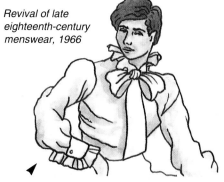

Different kinds of clothes are called styles. Because they are often only popular for a short while, they are also called fashions. If a fashion from the past becomes popular again, it is called a revival or 'retro'.

Throughout the centuries, a gradual broadening out of fashionable taste can be traced, from the aristocrats through to the middle classes and then to working people. In earlier times, attitudes to clothes tended to differ between the classes. Aristocrats were mainly concerned with show, the middle classes with respectability and the working classes often wore uniforms or practical working clothes. ►

1953, queen

bank manager

newspaper seller

Since World War II, young people have had more money to spend and, through television and magazines, they are more aware of clothes. ▼

There have been many youth styles...

Teddy boy, 1958

Rocker, 1962

Mod, 1965

Hippy, 1969

Skinhead, 1971

Punk, 1977

Scientists agree that humans are related to the apes. Humans were once covered in hair. Then they began to migrate and had to adapt to different climates. Gradually, over many, many generations, humans grew finer and finer hair and became less 'furry', though nobody really knows why. This meant that when the weather was cold, humans were forced to find 'clothes' of fur to keep them warm.

◄ The human body is capable of adapting to extremes of heat and cold. For example, some of the native people of Tierra del Fuego, in the far south of South America, lived in a cold climate, yet did not wear clothes. They carried a sort of woven mat that they held on the side of the body facing the wind.

In ancient times, wealthy Greeks believed that only slaves and barbarians wore a lot of clothes. They thought that it was unhealthy in a hot climate. They often wore only a large oblong of white cloth called an epiblemata. This was draped and folded round the body. The loose cloth sheltered the wearer from the sun and helped cool air to flow round the body. ◄

SHOES AND BOOTS

For millions of years, people wore nothing on their feet. In some parts of the world, people still go barefoot. You could say they grow their own shoes. By walking or running on rough ground, they develop hard patches of skin called calluses, which make their feet tough.

As civilization developed, people from powerful families spent less and less time walking outdoors on rough ground. Their feet became tender, so when they did walk outside, their feet would hurt. In ancient Egypt, noblemen would walk barefoot, followed by a servant carrying their shoes, ready for when they were needed.

Shoes became a sign of importance. Egyptian slaves and peasants were discouraged from wearing them. Egyptian shoes were often made from reeds or leather. Tutankhamen's tomb contained sandals. Pictures of his enemies were drawn on the soles, so he could tread them underfoot.

In Africa, some people make shoes out of old car tyres.

Hot, enclosed feet often smell, so many people use insoles containing carbon granules to soak up smells.

In rainy countries, it's important to have shoes that keep out water. The problem is that most waterproof materials also keep out the air. Feet need to breathe through the pores or tiny holes in the skin. Animal skins provide a good material for shoes, particularly if the leather is treated or cured, making it both flexible and waterproof but also allowing air to pass through. Skins were traditionally cured in urine – there are now modern substitutes.

Balkan opanques are shoes with toe hooks. These are specially designed to grip the toe-bar provided on some non-Western toilets.

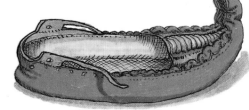

Modern wellies are made of rubber.

From ancient times, boots have been used by soldiers for protection when marching across rough or wet ground. Wellington boots were named after the Duke of Wellington and were originally made of leather. They became very fashionable for men in the nineteenth century. The longer the boot, the more important the wearer.

Clogs are wooden shoes that easily slip on and off the feet. They were popular in flat countries such as Holland and northern France, and with nineteenth-century British mill workers. In France, they are called sabots. People who threw their shoes into machines were called 'saboteurs'.

High heels have been fashionable since the nineteenth century. They are meant to give height and improve the shape of the calf. Stiletto heels, very popular in the 1950s, damaged floors because so much weight was centred on two tiny spots. A similar shoe was fashionable for men in the seventeenth century.

Galoshes are rubber overshoes that slip over ordinary footwear.

A pair of cloth gaiters wrapped around the leg above the shoe or boot formed another form of leg protection. These helped to keep legs and stockings dry and warm in winter and were especially popular in the English countryside from about 1790.

Sneakers are sports shoes with canvas uppers and rubber soles. They have steadily been replaced by trainers, which have leather or cloth uppers and air cushions in the sole. The cushions help protect the feet, legs and spine from injury.

Poulaines were long, pointed shoes worn in the Middle Ages. They had curling toes that could be up to 60 cm long and might be attached by strings to the knees.

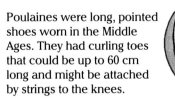

Winklepickers became fashionable in the early 1960s and got their name because they look like a tool for getting winkles out of their shells.

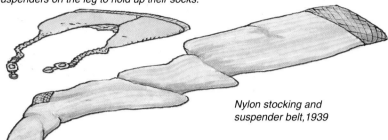

UNDERWEAR

It might be said that the first man or woman to wear one garment on top of another was the inventor of underwear. Now, we all use underwear to keep warm and clean, and sometimes to change the shape of our bodies.

Underwear helps to prevent dirt and smells from the body from reaching outer garments, which are normally thicker and harder to clean. Before the days of washing machines, people washed clothes by hand – scrubbing, rubbing, beating and shaking.

One of the simplest pieces of underwear for both men and women was the sleeved vest or undershirt. It hung from the shoulders and reached the hips or thighs.

Many men wear short-sleeved vests or singlets. However, in 1934, many American clothes shops reported a drop in vest sales after Clark Gable appeared without one in the film, *It Happened One Night*.

The T-shirt originated in America and was a simply-shaped vest. It is now worn as an outer garment by both sexes. It became fashionable after Marlon Brando wore one in the 1951 film, *A Streetcar Named Desire*.

The modern bra, or brassiere, was invented in France in 1912. It was formed from two handkerchieves and was often used to keep the body flat, because the new, working, professional women of the 1920s preferred a more boyish style of dressing.

At first bras were not firmly shaped. From 1936, however, semi-circular stitching gave the breasts a clearer shape. Wartime films began to show women with larger breasts. The film producer Howard Hughes designed a special bra for actress Jane Russell to wear during the filming of The Outlaw in 1943. It made her breasts stick out more. The bra helped another actress, Lana Turner, to show off the shape of her body in close-fitting sweaters. She became known as the 'sweater girl'.

Younger girls in the 1950s, however, found freedom with simple liberty bodices. In the 1960s, some of the new feminists burnt their bras as a protest against fashions which seemed designed only to please men.

In the 1980s, the singer Madonna wore a sharply pointed bra on the outside of her clothes to proclaim a more confident type of woman.

Corsets are designed to give women narrow waists. Sometimes men wear them too, either because they want to look slimmer or because they want to support a weak back. In the nineteenth century, women's waists were sometimes squeezed down to 45 cm, which caused breathing difficulties, frequent fainting, crushed ribs and even death from damaged lungs.

In the nineteenth century, women were considered beautiful if they were S-shaped when viewed from the side. To achieve this, women needed their bottoms to stick out. They wore bustles (a sort of padded frame around the hips and bottom), sometimes adding crinolines – cage-like petticoats that made the dresses on top spread out. The tight-fitting corset helped to control the shape of women's breasts – flattening them or pushing them upwards.

Until the late 1930s, when Y-fronts appeared, men often wore long underpants of silk or linen. Pants, or panties, and briefs are now common for men and women, while men also wear boxer shorts.

Men and women used to wear linen drawers, or from the nineteenth century, the longer bloomers. Originally these were two separate tubes of cloth. French knickers, loose-fitting and fastened with a button, came into fashion in the 1920s. Sometimes they would fall down. It was said to be a sign of a true lady that if they did fall down she could carry on walking as if nothing had happened.

SKIRTS AND SARIS

Skirts have been worn throughout history, often by men as well as women. They are often shaped to fit the body, though some are simply wrapped around the waist.

Arabian haik

South Indian dhoti

Malaysian sarong

Many garments in warm countries simply wrap around the body. Such simple garments are easy to adjust and look elegant and dignified. Although the garments themselves are simple, great care is often taken over the kind of material used, the beauty of the pattern and the way it is wrapped and folded. Skirts are still worn by men as well as women in many hot countries. They are cooler than trousers, because air can circulate between the legs.

The Indian sari has been worn for at least a thousand years. It covers most of a woman's body, going right round the trunk and then over the shoulder, and sometimes over the head. The material is usually more than five metres long and over a metre wide. The Malaysian sarong is similar but is worn by men from the waist, and by women from the waist or the breasts down to the ankles.

Punk, 1977

Greek guard's costume

Scottish kilt

The Scottish or Irish kilt is really a short kind of sarong, made of thick woollen plaid, and containing many pleats. Other European men also wear skirts – guardsmen in the Greek army and a few modern city dwellers, such as the punks, who dress to shock.

Skirt lengths have changed frequently over the years. Rich women tended to wear longer skirts, while working women wore shorter skirts because they were more practical.

Skirt lengths tend to get shorter at times when women have more work, more money to spend and are more adventurous as, for example, in the 1920s and the 1960s.

English lady and peasant, 1350

1905

1925

1955

1965

The fishtail skirt (1877-1888) was so tight that an ankle-chain had to be worn to stop the wearer from taking large steps and splitting the skirt. Really fashionable women wore a chamois-leather undergarment beneath it, which allowed the knees to move only a few centimetres. It is not surprising that the fashion only lasted a few years.

Fishtail skirt

A man trying to shake hands with a woman in 1856 might have had difficulty.

Men and women have often tried to look as different to each other as possible. In the nineteenth century women took to wearing enormous skirts and dresses to exaggerate their femininity.

During World War II, short skirts in a simple, straight cut were worn by women who had to help the war effort and save on materials.

Local materials were once used to make clothes. Dresses made from tree bark were worn by some native Americans. Grass skirts are worn on some South Pacific islands.

Grass skirt

Long trains were fashionable around the beginning of the twentieth century but they collected a lot of dirt as they brushed along the ground.

Soon after World War II, the French designer Christian Dior created a sensation with his 'New Look'. This featured wide, full-length skirts that were extravagant with material.

The short, straight skirts of the 1920s were a sign of women's growing independence. Short skirts shocked some old-fashioned people, who thought that women should remain covered up, and that short skirts were indecent. In Utah in the United States, women who wore skirts higher than 8 cm above the ankle could be imprisoned. In Italy, the Archbishop of Naples suggested that the earthquake at Amalfi was a punishment from heaven for those people who wore skirts that skimmed the knee.

In the 1960s, ordinary skirts first climbed above the knee and then rapidly shot up to the the thigh with the arrival of the mini skirt. When the model Jean Shrimpton, known as 'The Shrimp', appeared at the Melbourne Gold Cup horse race in a mini skirt in 1965, she caused a sensation. The popularity of the mini skirt was helped by the wearing of tights, which kept the top of the leg covered up. When the 1960s ended, skirt lengths fell rapidly.

1927: Oxford bags were wide flannel trousers worn by fashionable young men. The trouser bottoms could measure up to 120 cm round.

1956: drainpipe trousers were cut as narrow as possible.

1967: hipsters, or loons, were narrow and hung low on the hips.

1970: flares, or bell bottoms, were almost a revival of Oxford bags.

WHO WEARS THE TROUSERS?

Trousers have traditionally been worn by men, and men in the past have had more power than women in most societies. Trousers came to mean masculinity and therefore authority. The question 'Who wears the trousers?' used to mean which member of the family is in charge – the husband or the wife?

Breeches or knickerbockers were worn with stockings between the sixteenth and the eighteenth centuries.

Originally, men's trousers had a flap with buttons that came down in front, but this was replaced by the button fly. In the 1930s, the zip fly was worn by the trend-setting Edward, Prince of Wales.

Jeans are the most famous trousers of all. The cloth is a cotton twill, usually blue, which was once made in France. The name denim comes from the French for 'of Nîmes', a French town. Originally made as working men's trousers in the California gold rush, denim jeans are now a universal uniform of youth.

Zips were first used in America to fasten boots. For many years they were unpopular because they were unreliable but by 1918 they were used on flying suits and later on galoshes.

Trousers were worn by the nomads and horsemen of Asia to protect their legs from the cold and stop them getting sore while riding. These trousers probably developed from animal skins that were tied around the legs with thongs.

Many Persian, North Indian and Far Eastern women wear trousers.

Bloomers were an early attempt at women's trousers. They were invented by Amelia Bloomer in 1851 in the interests of health and comfort. She thought them more 'rational' than skirts. ▶

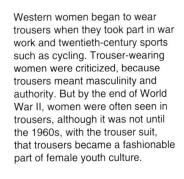

Vietnamese woman

Western women began to wear trousers when they took part in war work and twentieth-century sports such as cycling. Trouser-wearing women were criticized, because trousers meant masculinity and authority. But by the end of World War II, women were often seen in trousers, although it was not until the 1960s, with the trouser suit, that trousers became a fashionable part of female youth culture.

The ancient Romans, in their dignified togas, thought trousers rather barbaric. They only began wearing them after they came into contact with the Celtic and Germanic tribes of the north. Trousers offered better protection against the weather than togas or leather skirts.

In the Middle Ages, men wore hose, a tube-like garment halfway between tights and today's trousers. It was warm and flexible. Around the the same time men started to wear short puffy trousers, gathered at the thigh. They held their hose up by tying it to their shirts with laces called points. ◀

After the French Revolution, members of French high society wore long trousers with wide bottoms adopted from the dress of British sailors.

▼

Turn-ups appeared on the bottom of trousers at the end of the nineteenth century. It is said that this trend was started by an Englishman in the United States. He was caught in the rain and late for a wedding, so he turned up his trousers to keep them dry at the bottom, and forgot to turn them down again.

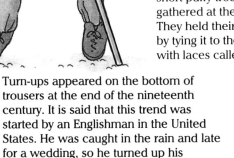

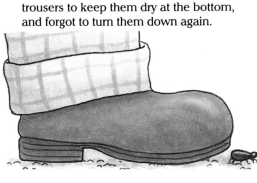

In the late eighteenth century, braces came into use. They kept the front of the breeches smooth and they probably felt comfortable to wear after a large dinner.

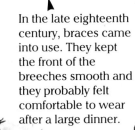

Some sports require special, protective clothing. The first practical aqualung system was devised by Jacques Cousteau and Émile Gagnan in 1943. When added to a pair of flippers, a face mask and a streamlined diving suit, modern scuba diving was born.

In some sports, players wear bright clothes, sometimes of a special team design, so that team members can be identified. Numbers on the shirt also identify the player. Fans sometimes wear team shirts to show which football club they support.

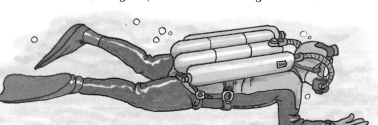

LOOKING SPORTY

Sport has given us many different kinds of clothes. When a sport is new, people tend to use whatever clothes are available, but as time goes by they start to use special items of clothing.

At the beginning of the twentieth century, it was considered indecent to expose too much flesh. Long skirts were worn by women for bathing, cycling, and tennis. However, skirts gradually became much shorter. In 1949, "Gorgeous" Gussie Moran became famous for the short tennis skirts and frilly knickers she wore when she played at Wimbledon.

Sportswear can be attractive enough to wear in everyday life. This is why tennis shoes, jogging suits, baseball caps, and boxer shorts are worn as fashion clothes.

Women's swimming suits used to cover all of the body. They grew shorter and shorter leading eventually to the skimpy two-piece bikini of the 1950s. Strangely enough, a garment like this was originally used by girl gymnasts in Roman times, while ancient Egyptian girl acrobats wore only a loin cloth.

Some materials, such as lycra and sweatshirts, have also come from the world of sport into general use. Sweatshirts are designed to keep you warm when your body cools with sweat. Lycra is an artificial material made from oil. It both stretches and returns to its original shape, keeping a warm, close, comfortable fit.

In sports where people need to move quickly, they use a few, light, close-fitting articles of clothing. The ancient Greeks, who invented the Olympic Games, competed completely naked. These days, some track athletes wear streamlined clothes originally designed for cyclists.

Old-fashioned gear

In some sports, people are still wearing clothes that were fashionable when the sport first became popular. That's why baseball players wear nineteenth-century knickerbockers and socks, for example.

Golf has been played since the 1600s, but it became very popular in the 1920s, and so some of today's golfers wear typical 1920s leisure styles – sweaters, caps, and sometimes knickers.

Protective gear

Atheletes have developed a wide range of protective gear, including leg pads, gloves, and helmets.

Horse riders often wear long boots, breeches or jodhpurs, and a hard hat. Riding breeches are tight at the knee, so the rider can easily grip and guide the horse.

Each of the fighting sports has its own protective clothing. Boxers wear shoes, shorts, and padded mittens, known as boxing gloves. These gloves were introduced by the Marquess of Queensberry in the nineteenth century to make boxing safer.

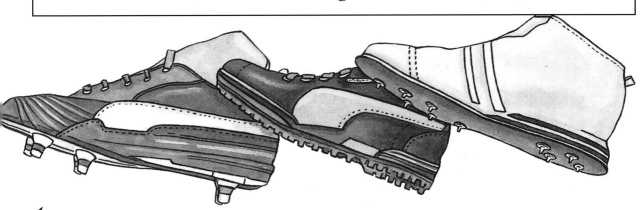

Different sports require different footwear for keeping a grip on the playing surface. Soccer players use different kinds of cleats according to the field. Sprinters use spikes, which were invented by the Romans for marching on rough ground. Some high jumpers use one shoe with spikes and one without.

JACKETS, SHIRTS AND WAISTCOATS

The modern jacket with a collared shirt and tie beneath, and possibly a waistcoat, is almost like a uniform for Western men. Modern-looking short jackets first appeared in the 1920s. They still retain features from earlier periods that have little use nowadays. ►

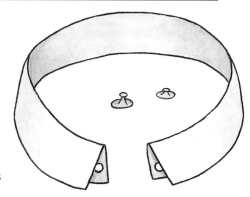

In the 1980s, some women started to wear jackets with padded shoulders. The jackets make women look broader and consequently stronger, maybe helping them to compete with men in business. Clothes with broad shoulders were also worn by women at the turn of this century and during World War II to assert women's equality with men in the workplace.

1900

1943

1985

Button Box

Right- and left-handed buttons: most people are right-handed so men who dressed themselves preferred a button on the right. Wealthy women, on the other hand, were once dressed by their servants, and so buttoning on the left (that is, the servant's right) was more convenient. Button positions have remained ever since.

The lapel buttonhole: coats once buttoned at the neck. People now use it to wear flowers, such as carnations.

The collar slit: collars used to be so high that they would not lie down flat when folded over, unless cut with a slit.

Cuff buttons: cuffs used to be so wide that they had to be buttoned back to stay in place.

A shirt is a type of vest, usually with buttons, which is designed to be seen. It is an ancient garment which has appeared at other times and places, often in longer form, as the tunic (Roman), the caftan (Africa and the East) and the kimono (Japan).

When worn with a coat, some parts of the shirt show at the neck or the sleeves. These parts tend to get dirty, and so, originally, shirt collars and cuffs were separate items that could be changed easily, without having to change the shirt as well.

One cause of the French Revolution, 1789-99, was the extravagant lifestyle of the aristocrats. Because many aristocrats could be recognized by their expensive clothes and had their heads chopped off, it became safer to dress less conspicuously.

Beau Brummel set a new standard of sober elegance for society. The shape of his Regency coat had a great influence on English men's fashion.

Bankers and industrialists needed to look reliable in a rapidly changing world. Their dress became even more sober as the nineteenth century wore on.

Long waistcoats with long sleeves were first worn in the 1660s. They were cut just like the long coat of the time, but more tightly, so another, open coat could be worn over them. In the eighteenth century, elaborately embroidered waistcoats could reach down to the knee. Today, only the short waistcoat survives, normally as part of a three-piece suit. Sometimes a lavishly coloured silk waistcoat is still worn.

For most of European history, men's fashions were often more splendid than women's, just as among animals the males are often more brightly coloured than the females. The modern, sober style of dress for men was introduced in the nineteenth century.

In cold weather a long- or short-sleeved pullover may be worn over the shirt, and under a jacket. Pullovers are really just overshirts made of wool for warmth.

Pullover, 1935

American bomber jacket, 1945

Anorak, 1960

If you want to show that you belong in a certain group, you can wear a blazer – striped or just one colour, often with a badge on the breast pocket. They are thought to have been worn first by the crew of the Royal Navy ship HMS *Blazer* in 1845.

The leather, fleece-lined jacket worn by World War II bomber crews has made a big impact on post-war styles. The bomber jacket was redesigned by motorcyclists, and the new biker's jacket was made famous by Marlon Brando in the 1954 film *The Wild One*. The grubby leather jacket is now often seen as a symbol of youthful rebellion.

Anoraks were originally Inuit garments made of seal skin.

SUIT YOURSELF

Today's suit was an invention of the twentieth century, though its origins were much earlier. By the 1920s, men were no longer expected to express themselves in their dress. Individual tailoring went into decline. Men began to buy their suits more cheaply with 'off the peg' standard designs.

By the middle of the nineteenth century, men's outerwear had settled down to three main pieces – a cut-away coat, a waistcoat and the newly adopted trousers. At first, the three pieces would be of different colours, favourites for everyday wear being London Fog, Algerian Dust and Russian Green. But after 1850, only the waistcoat remained colourful. The age of the businessman had begun and sober colours reflected the sombre style of the City of London.

Business suit, 1960

Business suit, 1870

Since World War II, the grey suit has been increasingly restricted to business and formal wear. The English man's suit, as designed by Hardy Amies and manufactured in Savile Row, remains a classic.

In the 1980s, the Milan-based designer, Giorgio Armani, began to produce looser, baggier suits. They could be worn with the sleeves pushed up, as by pop star George Michael.

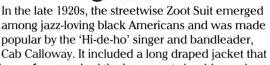

In the late 1920s, the streetwise Zoot Suit emerged among jazz-loving black Americans and was made popular by the 'Hi-de-ho' singer and bandleader, Cab Calloway. It included a long draped jacket that reached the knee, vast shoulder pads and baggy trousers that tapered at the turn-ups. It was worn with pointed shoes, a broad-brimmed hat, a lengthy, dangling key-chain and long greased-back hair.

The Zazou fashion of post-war Paris was based on the Zoot Suit but had drooping shoulders and tight trousers. In the 1950s, the Teddy Boy style continued the draped coat tradition, but added thick crêpe-soled shoes and, for the hair, a quiff, swept-back sides and sideburns. Teddy girls wore less distinctive clothes but were recognizable by their pony tails.

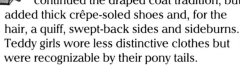

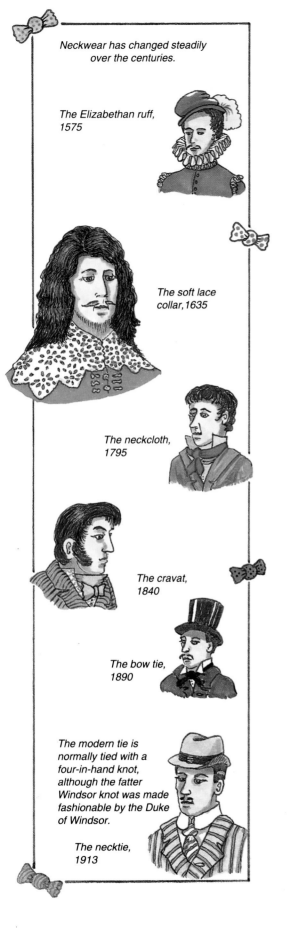

Neckwear has changed steadily over the centuries.

The Elizabethan ruff, 1575

The soft lace collar, 1635

The neckcloth, 1795

The cravat, 1840

The bow tie, 1890

The modern tie is normally tied with a four-in-hand knot, although the fatter Windsor knot was made fashionable by the Duke of Windsor.

The necktie, 1913

Around 1800, Beau Brummel, the leader of Regency fashion, advised the Prince Regent to wear black or dark blue coats for evening wear. Evening knee-breeches were already usually black at that time, so when trousers were introduced they too were black. The black evening suit was born. By about 1870, the full evening dress tail-coat suit was well established. These days, the long-tailed evening dress suit is normally only worn by posh waiters. However, a similar morning dress survives at modern weddings, though these suits are usually coloured light grey.

Today's short, modern dinner jacket came into use at the start of the twentieth century. For a time it was thought too informal for dining out, because tail-coats were still worn. By the 1920s, however, short jackets were accepted for formal evening wear.

In the late nineteenth century an attempt was made to go back to the fancier clothes of earlier times. The 'Little Lord Fauntleroy' suit worn by some nineteenth-century children was based on Thomas Gainsborough's 1770 painting, *The Blue Boy*. Oscar Wilde tried to popularize it as men's wear and wore it on a tour of America, but it didn't catch on.

49

POSH DRESSES

Original tailored dresses are very expensive, but designers also create simpler, less expensive versions which they sell 'off the peg' in dress shops under their own labels. This trend followed the mass-market success of popular designers such as Mary Quant in the 1960s.

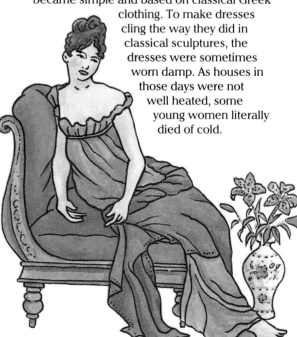

Court dress, 1865

Wedding dress worn by Lady Diana Spencer, 1981

For hundreds of years, until early in the twentieth century, women's dresses generally grew more and more lavish, getting larger, more complex, and using more and more material. Women not only wanted to look more attractive but also to show off their wealth and position.

In the Middle Ages in Europe, dresses were still fairly simple. Fabric was expensive and status was shown by the cost of the material, fur trim or jewels that went with it. It was against the law in some countries for lower class people to wear expensive clothing.

By the fifteenth century, the skirts of dresses were made so long and full they had to be held up as the lady moved. This resulted in a big bunching of material in front so that the woman often looked as if she was pregnant even when she wasn't.

Late in the sixteenth century, women started wearing various types of structure under the skirt, such as bumrolls, bustles or crinolines. This meant that even more material could be used but the wearer could still just about move with them.

The French Revolution not only abolished the monarchy but also the extravagant style of dresses of the French royal court. Clothes became simple and based on classical Greek clothing. To make dresses cling the way they did in classical sculptures, the dresses were sometimes worn damp. As houses in those days were not well heated, some young women literally died of cold.

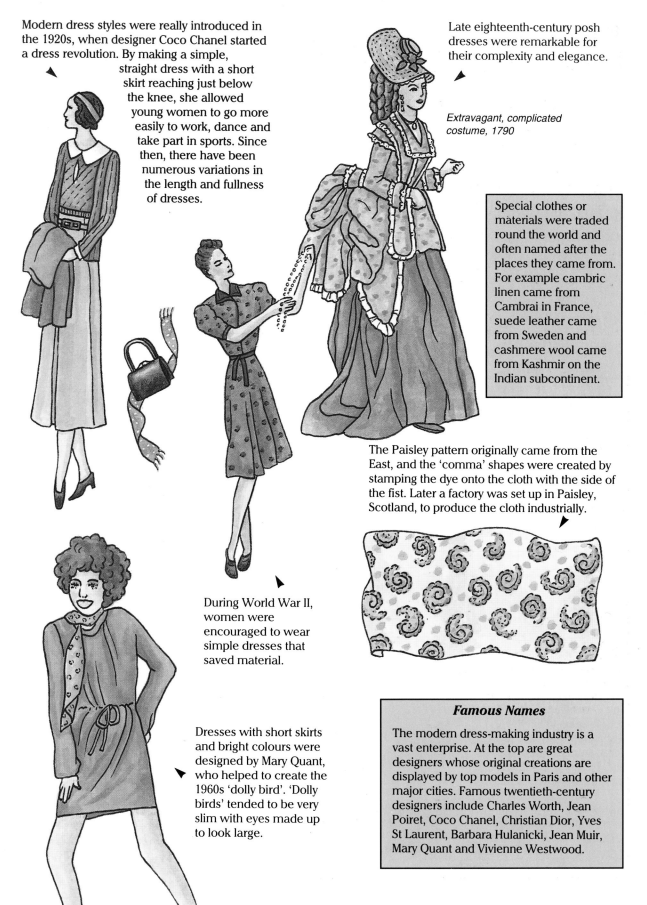

Modern dress styles were really introduced in the 1920s, when designer Coco Chanel started a dress revolution. By making a simple, straight dress with a short skirt reaching just below the knee, she allowed young women to go more easily to work, dance and take part in sports. Since then, there have been numerous variations in the length and fullness of dresses.

Late eighteenth-century posh dresses were remarkable for their complexity and elegance.

Extravagant, complicated costume, 1790

Special clothes or materials were traded round the world and often named after the places they came from. For example cambric linen came from Cambrai in France, suede leather came from Sweden and cashmere wool came from Kashmir on the Indian subcontinent.

The Paisley pattern originally came from the East, and the 'comma' shapes were created by stamping the dye onto the cloth with the side of the fist. Later a factory was set up in Paisley, Scotland, to produce the cloth industrially.

During World War II, women were encouraged to wear simple dresses that saved material.

Dresses with short skirts and bright colours were designed by Mary Quant, who helped to create the 1960s 'dolly bird'. 'Dolly birds' tended to be very slim with eyes made up to look large.

Famous Names

The modern dress-making industry is a vast enterprise. At the top are great designers whose original creations are displayed by top models in Paris and other major cities. Famous twentieth-century designers include Charles Worth, Jean Poiret, Coco Chanel, Christian Dior, Yves St Laurent, Barbara Hulanicki, Jean Muir, Mary Quant and Vivienne Westwood.

UNIFORMS

A uniform makes a group of otherwise quite different individuals look similar. It is a simple way to make sure that everyone in a group is dressed both smartly and suitably. It also helps us to know what people do. For instance, if someone becomes seriously ill at a football match, someone who can help needs to be found quickly. That's why ambulance staff wear a uniform that people will recognize.

Until the middle of the last century, many soldiers wore brightly-coloured uniforms. Red was popular because it is a bold, threatening colour and hides blood stains. Unfortunately bright colours made soldiers easy targets. In 1843, Harry Lumsden, a British officer in India, issued his men in the Queen's Own Corps of Guides with cotton clothing dyed grey with mazari, a local plant. The leather items were dyed with mulberry juice to produce a drab yellow shade, called 'khaki' after the local word for dust. In 1849, these Guides, known as 'mudlarks', were seen in battle for the first time. Except for ceremonial occasions, most soldiers now wear dull colours or camouflage uniforms.

US Army jungle camouflage uniform, 1945

Military uniforms may include elements designed to make the soldier look fiercer. Hats and vertical stripes make people seem taller. Fur and feather head-dresses suggest a fierce animal with its hair on end. Frogging or gold braid in rows across the body may have come from an ancient custom of going into battle painted like a skeleton to scare the enemy.

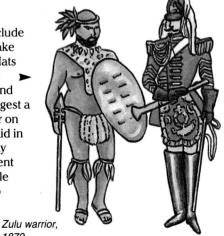

Zulu warrior, 1879

Trumpeter, French Imperial Guard, 1810

A uniform can give the idea that the wearer is prepared to serve others. Because the uniform makes the wearer more anonymous we may find it easier to ask them to do things for us. That is one reason why shop assistants often wear special clothes.

Different military ranks wear different uniforms or insignia so that an easily recognized chain of command is maintained. Chevrons are worn on the arm by some British Army ranks. ▼

Staff sergeant *Sergeant* *Corporal* *Lance corporal* *Private*

Dungaree was a coarse, Indian blue, calico material used for sails. After a bad storm, sailors sometimes used any ripped sails to make new trousers. This became part of a sailor's outfit. With the addition of a bib in front, they became the modern form of dungarees. ►

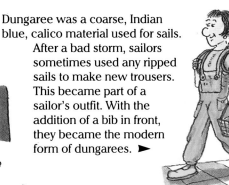

In the Middle Ages, doctors wore gowns of blue and red to hide the blood. Today the academic gowns worn in some universities still preserve these colours, as well as the medieval gown, hood or cap.

Before the introduction of ► purpose-built hospitals, nursing was often performed by nuns. The traditional nurse's uniforms are developed from the nuns' cape, cloak and headwear.

Parlourmaid, 1893

Nurse, 1905

Augustinian nursing sister, 1256

The traditional posh waitress's uniform of black with a white apron is a development of the nineteenth-century parlourmaid's outfit.

School uniforms in many parts of the world are based on the English boarding-school uniforms of the 1920s. They often include blazers with a badge. Some boys still wear caps, whereas girls wear round felt or straw hats. ►

Traditional school uniforms

53

OVERCOATS AND GLOVES

The overcoat is an answer to an age-old problem – what to wear if you go out in rainy or cold weather. Wearing thick clothes was fine but if they were wet through you would either have to sit in them when you got home or change them. With an overcoat, you could simply take the outer garment off.

The first overcoats were long, cut-away jackets made of tough material. During the eighteenth century, coach travel became more and more commonplace. People who rode on top were exposed to the weather for long periods. They needed heavy great-coats with large collars.

By the beginning of the eighteenth century, women in England were able to wear lightweight walking coats outside their simpler, straighter gowns. Soon the race was on to develop a truly waterproof coat.

Charles Macintosh was a nineteenth-century chemist who produced a kind of waterproof smock lined with rubber. This was called a mackintosh. Early mackintoshes sometimes smelled very bad and caused offense.

Some modern mackintoshes are made of transparent plastic and bright, shiny PVC. Increasingly, people are wearing shorter types of rainwear as, with modern transport, they do not expect to be in bad weather much of the time.

Barbour coat

In the eighteenth century, waterproofs were made of tarpaulin (sail-cloth coated with tar), or oil-cloth (a cloth coated with boiled linseed oil). Today's Barbour country coat is descended from these first waterproof coats.

Fur has been worn from earliest times for warmth, and also as a luxury item. It is less popular today as many people think that animals should not die to provide luxurious clothes for people.

The modern anorak, or parka, was originally an Inuit garment made from fur turned inside out for warmth. For a fully waterproof garment, the Inuit cured fish skins and sewed them together.

The cape or cloak was simple and could be worn easily on horseback. One version of the cape that is widely worn today is the South American poncho, a blanket used by gaucho cowboys.

Glove Box

Gloves were an important item of clothing in the Middle Ages and often had a symbolic value. To give your hand or glove meant to pledge your loyalty, while throwing your glove at an enemy was a way of challenging him or her to a duel.

In the sixteenth and seventeenth centuries, richly embroidered gloves were given as valuable presents.

Women began to wear shorter-sleeved dresses in the 1630s, but they also wore gloves that reached the elbow.

Another way of keeping warm is to wear a muff. By the eighteenth century, muffs had grown big enough to carry lap-dogs in and were sometimes worn by men. They became an important fashion accessory and by 1880, muffs were sometimes worn with the heads of owls or squirrels attached. Some were made of the entire body of a kitten!

During the late nineteenth century it was thought indecent for women to show too much skin. They would often wear lace or net gloves – even indoors.

55

For hundreds of years in many parts of the world, fair skin was the mark of a lady of leisure. It proved that she didn't have to work outside in the sunlight. In the twentieth century this has changed. A tanned skin is evidence of a long sunny holiday. It has become a sign of wealth, and so is thought attractive. This is why some people wear fake suntan, or lie under a sun-lamp, to look darker. On the other hand, it is now known that too much exposure to the Sun can cause skin cancer and it is no longer thought unfashionable to have white skin.

From Roman times, European ladies have used special substances to whiten their skins. However, in the sixteenth century, rouge was also applied to add colour to the cheeks.

The ancient Egyptians used both orange and yellow face paints. Egyptian women liked to look light and so tended to use yellow; Egyptian men wanted to look dark and so used only orange. Cleopatra also used varnish on her nails.

MAKE-UP, HAIR AND TATTOOS

Even the finest clothes don't make a person happy if he or she thinks there's something wrong with the way they look. People have always gone to great lengths to change their eyes, lips, skin and hair.

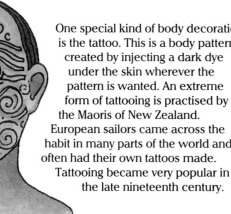

One special kind of body decoration is the tattoo. This is a body pattern created by injecting a dark dye under the skin wherever the pattern is wanted. An extreme form of tattooing is practised by the Maoris of New Zealand. European sailors came across the habit in many parts of the world and often had their own tattoos made. Tattooing became very popular in the late nineteenth century.

Celtic warrior, 55 BC

Maori face tattoos

Tattoos don't show up well on people with very dark skin so they use the keloid or scarring technique. This is a common practice in Africa. The skin is cut or pierced repeatedly, then left to heal, leaving a slightly raised scar pattern.

The Celts, who lived in much of western Europe, used to decorate their bodies. When Julius Caesar arrived in Britain, he found that Celtic warriors sometimes painted themselves with a blue vegetable dye called woad. This may have been to protect themselves magically or to make them look frightening.

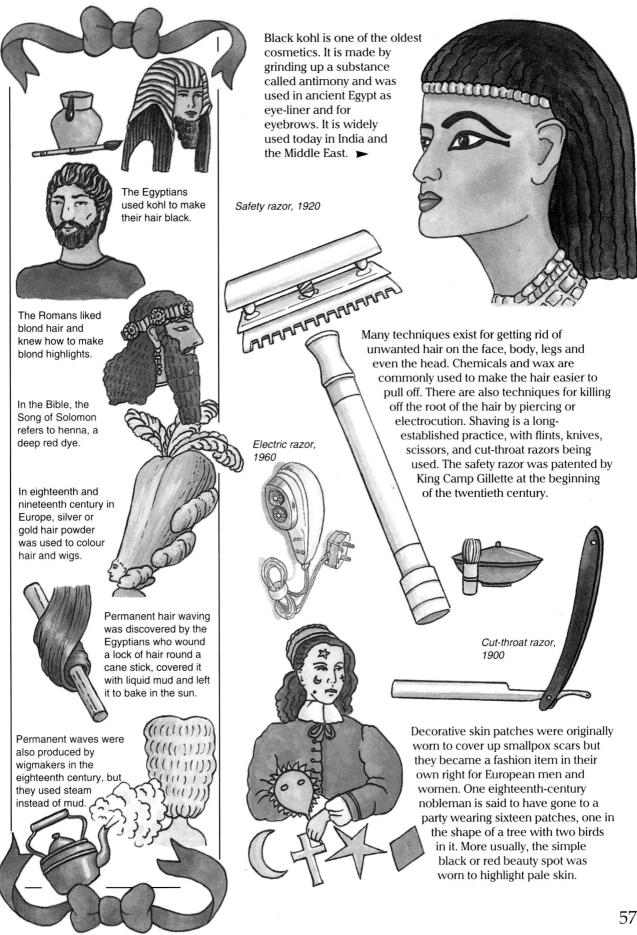

The Egyptians used kohl to make their hair black.

Black kohl is one of the oldest cosmetics. It is made by grinding up a substance called antimony and was used in ancient Egypt as eye-liner and for eyebrows. It is widely used today in India and the Middle East. ►

Safety razor, 1920

The Romans liked blond hair and knew how to make blond highlights.

In the Bible, the Song of Solomon refers to henna, a deep red dye.

In eighteenth and nineteenth century in Europe, silver or gold hair powder was used to colour hair and wigs.

Electric razor, 1960

Many techniques exist for getting rid of unwanted hair on the face, body, legs and even the head. Chemicals and wax are commonly used to make the hair easier to pull off. There are also techniques for killing off the root of the hair by piercing or electrocution. Shaving is a long-established practice, with flints, knives, scissors, and cut-throat razors being used. The safety razor was patented by King Camp Gillette at the beginning of the twentieth century.

Permanent hair waving was discovered by the Egyptians who wound a lock of hair round a cane stick, covered it with liquid mud and left it to bake in the sun.

Cut-throat razor, 1900

Permanent waves were also produced by wigmakers in the eighteenth century, but they used steam instead of mud.

Decorative skin patches were originally worn to cover up smallpox scars but they became a fashion item in their own right for European men and women. One eighteenth-century nobleman is said to have gone to a party wearing sixteen patches, one in the shape of a tree with two birds in it. More usually, the simple black or red beauty spot was worn to highlight pale skin.

JEWELS AND THINGS

People have been using ornaments, umbrellas and handbags for thousands of years. Personal ornaments are probably an older tradition than clothes. Why do we decorate ourselves in this way? Is it to look beautiful or wealthy? Or for reasons of magic, religion or superstition? Sometimes it is simply because we need to carry something useful with us!

Jewels are made from attractive stones or metals that are often of great value because they are hard to find. Rare jewels show how rich the wearer is.

Some people suffer great discomfort for their ideas of beauty. In one African tribe, women stretch the neck by placing as many neck-rings as possible around it. This is because a long neck is often considered a sign of beauty. Neck-stretching is also practised in Myanmar (formerly Burma).

After the French Revolution, women offset their simple, low-cut dresses by wearing a red ribbon around the neck. This was a reference to the guillotine, the machine that was used to cut off the heads of the king's supporters.

The ancient Aztecs of Central America wore nose and ear ornaments made of gold. When attending festivals, they wore face paints and stamped patterns on their cheeks.

In medieval and Tudor times, heavy gold chains and ropes of pearls could be used as a substitute for money, with a length being broken off, weighed for its value and used as cash. Jewellery of different kinds has been used as money in this way because it has value and yet is easy to carry.

Umbrellas and parasols have other uses besides keeping off the weather. In some Eastern and African countries they are displayed as a sign of the user's importance.

Burmese state umbrella, 1890

Chatelaine, 1850

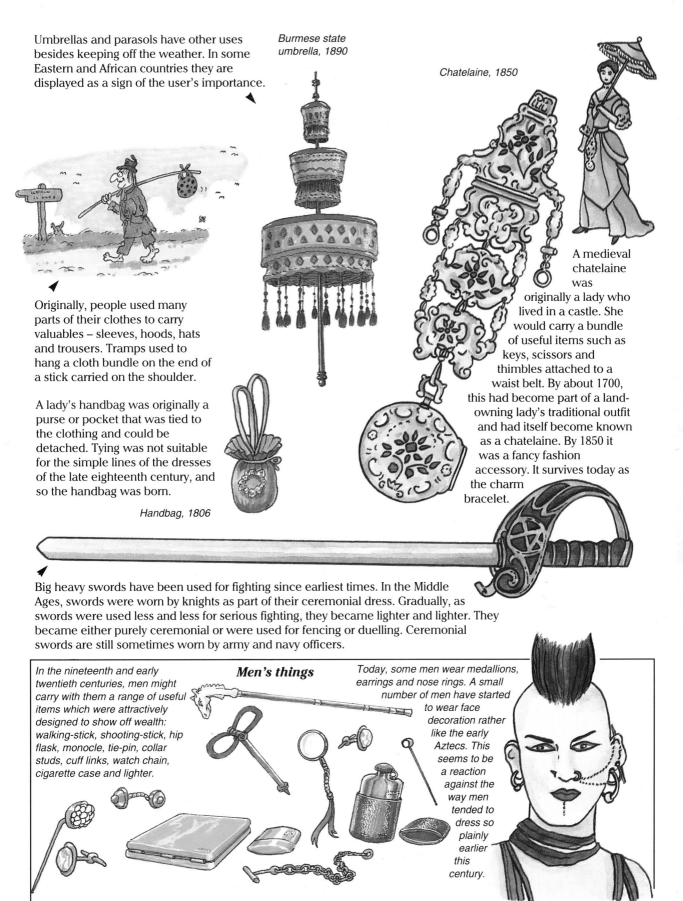

Originally, people used many parts of their clothes to carry valuables – sleeves, hoods, hats and trousers. Tramps used to hang a cloth bundle on the end of a stick carried on the shoulder.

A lady's handbag was originally a purse or pocket that was tied to the clothing and could be detached. Tying was not suitable for the simple lines of the dresses of the late eighteenth century, and so the handbag was born.

Handbag, 1806

A medieval chatelaine was originally a lady who lived in a castle. She would carry a bundle of useful items such as keys, scissors and thimbles attached to a waist belt. By about 1700, this had become part of a land-owning lady's traditional outfit and had itself become known as a chatelaine. By 1850 it was a fancy fashion accessory. It survives today as the charm bracelet.

Big heavy swords have been used for fighting since earliest times. In the Middle Ages, swords were worn by knights as part of their ceremonial dress. Gradually, as swords were used less and less for serious fighting, they became lighter and lighter. They became either purely ceremonial or were used for fencing or duelling. Ceremonial swords are still sometimes worn by army and navy officers.

Men's things

In the nineteenth and early twentieth centuries, men might carry with them a range of useful items which were attractively designed to show off wealth: walking-stick, shooting-stick, hip flask, monocle, tie-pin, collar studs, cuff links, watch chain, cigarette case and lighter.

Today, some men wear medallions, earrings and nose rings. A small number of men have started to wear face decoration rather like the early Aztecs. This seems to be a reaction against the way men tended to dress so plainly earlier this century.

Because hats are connected with power, men have often worn tall hats, and the more powerful the man, the larger the hat. People of lower status have usually worn smaller hats, taking them off in the presence of someone of higher rank. Traditionally, men also take off their hats in church and when meeting women. Women's hats are usually more decorative and fashionable than men's practical hats.

CHOOSING A HAT

Gentleman taking of his hat, 1908

Wimple

Yashmak

European women hardly wore hats at all until the sixteenth century. Headwear was often an elaborate veil or headscarf. In the Middle Ages, women wore a wimple – a piece of cloth covering the head. The wimple survives among nuns and nurses to the present day. Following upper class Greek practice in ancient Byzantium, many Muslim women now cover their faces with veils or face screens known as yashmaks.

Though baseball caps are popular these days, it's not fashionable in the West for men to wear traditional hats. In very cold or very hot weather, however, hats provide the wearer with shelter. They keep the head warm in winter and cool in summer.

Flat cap

Fez

Government regulations in Elizabethan times said that middle-ranking men should wear flat caps – a tradition that continued until the mid-twentieth century among working class men.

In some Muslim countries, men have worn turbans in a great variety of styles. Some have been copied by women in the West as fashion items. Some Muslim men also wear the fez, although in the 1920s this was banned in Turkey as part of an effort to make Turkey more Westernized.

The Mad Hatter's hat, 1865

Felt is a material made by soaking and compressing wool or fur so that the fibres bind together

into a kind of matting. It is often used to make hats because it can be shaped easily. The best felt used to come from old and sweaty beaver furs that had been worn by Russian noblemen.

In the eighteenth century, hat makers started to use mercuric nitrate as part of the felt-making process, without realizing that it was a poison. As a result, many hatters became mentally ill because their nerves were affected. Lewis Carroll, the author of *Alice in Wonderland*, based the character of the Mad Hatter on this affliction.

Hats come in all shapes and sizes.

The wide brim of the Mexican sombrero provides enough shade to cover the whole body.

The big, woolly hats worn by some Rastafarians keep their hair covered and bunched.

The balaclava is named after the woolly head-covers knitted for British soldiers who fought in the Battle of Balaklava, 1854.

The boater is a flat straw hat worn in the Victorian period by people who went boating on summer afternoons.

The Lapland bonnet has four pointed corners. Three can be stuffed with feathers for use as a pillow and the other used as a pocket or a purse.

Hat Box

A range of brimmed hats were worn by men in the nineteenth and early twentieth centuries.

Top hat

Stetson

Trilby

Bowler

Homburg

A beret is a felt cap commonly worn by peasants in the Basque areas of France and Spain. It became very popular as sportswear with both sexes in the early twentieth century but is now often associated with artists.

In the Australian bush, corks dangling from hat brims help to keep the flies away.

61

Men sometimes wear small hair pieces, or toupees, to disguise baldness. They are mostly knotted to a piece of netting and fixed to the scalp with double-sided tape.

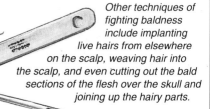

Other techniques of fighting baldness include implanting live hairs from elsewhere on the scalp, weaving hair into the scalp, and even cutting out the bald sections of the flesh over the skull and joining up the hairy parts.

WIGS

Some people wear wigs because they are bald – but that's never been the only reason for wearing them. Quite often people like to wear wigs for reasons of fashion. They are especially handy when the hairstyle required is a complicated one. Wigs can be made from human hair or from artificial fibres.

In the seventeenth and eighteenth centuries, the wig became an essential item for fashionable men and women. Its height and complexity increased to absurd proportions.

Afro wigs imitated a black hairstyle. In the late 1960s, it was popular with some white people who wanted to show solidarity with the struggle for black civil rights.

Roman women's fashion demanded a wardrobe of wigs. Golden Germanic hair was very popular.

The ancient Egyptians shaved their heads for coolness, but wore heavy wigs on formal occasions.

English lawyers still use wigs of the eighteenth-century style.

Toupee – or not toupee!

In eighteenth-century Europe, wigs became so popular that it was dangerous for children to go out alone in case their hair was cut off and stolen. Some bold thieves even stole expensive wigs!

Willy and Wanda have been invited to a '1796 Fancy Dress Ball'. Unfortunately the fancy dress shop has run out of the proper items. They each could only find three things worn in Europe in 1796. Do you know which they are?

WILLY AND WANDA'S
WACKYWEAR

QUIZ

Homburg

Balaclava

Beauty spot

Ruff

Necktie

T-shirt

Braces

Mackintosh smock

Roman skirt

Breeches

Wellies

Fez

Gold-powdered wig

Aqualung

Red neck-ribbon

Jacket with padded shoulders

Muffs

Bustle

Zip-up handbag

Fishtail skirt

Nylons

Poulaines

WHY DO WE USE THAT?

Alarm made from a bell in a candle. The bell fell out when the candle melted.

An early alarm using a candle flame to burn through a thread. When the thread broke the weight fell to the floor and made a noise.

In the 1851 Great Exhibition, Mr R W Savage exhibited a bed which woke sleepers with a bell, took off the blankets, tilted the mattress, and threw the sleeper on to the floor.

A CLEAN START

This book is all about the things we use and why we use them. Let's start in the bathroom...

Sponge

Real sponges are the skeletons of marine animals called sea sponges. Because they are soft and absorb water they are useful for washing with. Nowadays, most sponges are artificial.

Bathtubs help to maintain a person's privacy while he or she is washing. The first known bath was used in 1700 BC and was from ancient Crete. It looked remarkably like a nineteenth-century bath.

Soap dissolves dirt on skin and loosens grease. It was first used by German tribes in the first century AD and was made with a mixture of wood ashes and tallow (animal fat).

Loofahs are the fibre skeletons of marrow-like plants from North Africa. They are good for scrubbing away dead skin.

Loofah

Olive oil

Strigils

Before soap was invented, the Romans cleaned themselves with olive oil. This, along with the dirt from their bodies, was scraped off using a strigil, or curved scraper.

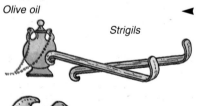

Ancient Indian razor

Nineteenth-century strop

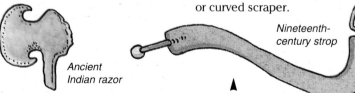

In some cultures men shave because a hairy face is seen as dirty or old-looking. Other cultures value beards as a sign of age and wisdom. Shaving was originally done with a special blade which was sharpened, or stropped, using a leather strop. Scalp hair was singed off with red-hot iron or coal, or it was plucked out by hand.

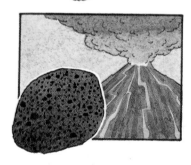

Pumice is volcanic rock which is naturally very rough. It is useful for scraping off ingrained dirt and dead skin.

If bits of food are left in the mouth, tooth enamel is likely to rot. In the past, people ate less sweet food than people do nowadays. Nevertheless, they needed to keep their teeth clean. The modern toothbrush was invented in 1780 by William Addis.

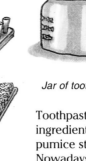

Jar of tooth powder

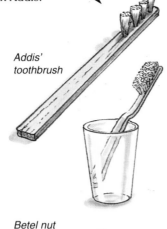

Addis' toothbrush

There are other ways to clean your teeth...

Use a toothpick

Chew a twig

Rub teeth with a cloth

Betel nut

Toothpaste was once made from ingredients such as powdered horn, pumice stone and charcoal. Nowadays one of the main ingredients is china clay. The tiny particles in toothpaste work in the same way as sandpaper, rubbing away the dirt from the teeth.

In India, people chew on betel nuts wrapped in pepper-vine leaves flavoured with lime. Chewing on betel nuts stimulates blood flow in the gums and hardens the teeth – though it also stains them black.

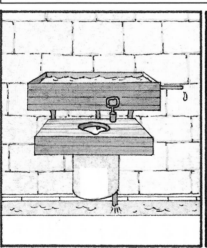

The first flush toilet was invented by Sir John Harington in 1596. One was installed in Richmond Palace for Queen Elizabeth I of England.

Garderobes were toilets built into the thick walls of castles and manor houses. They drained into the moat. Coats were kept in the garderobe because the ammonia from the urine kept away the larvae of moths which feed on cloth fibres.

Until late last century most people in England only had a toilet at the end of their garden, and used a chamber pot during the night. Some people had a cess-pit in the cellar.

Indian villagers often use a special area of woodland as a toilet. This practice is quite clean because the hot sun dries out the waste quickly.

In ancient Rome, buckets of salty water holding sponges on sticks were left in the public toilets – for communal use.

An astronaut has to keep a space suit on when space-walking. If he or she wants to go to the toilet, the urine is collected in a special bag and recycled as water to cool the suit.

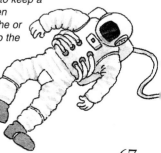

POTS AND PANS, TINS AND CANS

Cooking destroys some vitamins, especially those in fruits and vegetables. Because of this, some people choose to eat only raw food. But cooking also destroys dangerous bacteria and softens tough food. We could not easily eat grains like wheat and rice without cooking them. So on balance, cooking does more good than harm. Besides, cooked food tastes nice, which is the main reason why so many different foods and cooking equipment have been invented.

▲ One of the earliest examples of fires used for cooking comes from a cave in China where a 500,000 year-old hearth has been found.

Cattle dung is often used for fuel where firewood is in short supply. The dung is made into slabs which burn very slowly, providing a steady cooking temperature.

The first crude gas cooker was introduced in 1812. Later, special burner rings were devised which, by allowing more air to mix with the gas, burned the gas more efficiently. The 'Regulo' oven thermostat was introduced on gas cookers in 1923 to regulate temperatures.

Over the centuries many women have been killed whilst cooking over open fires because their clothes caught fire. This was called hearth death.

Clay ovens called tandoors are used in some areas of India. The sides of the tandoor are used for cooking flat bread, known as naan, while meat is roasted over the fire. This arrangement saves on scarce fuel.

▲ Cookers and radar may not seem to be related, but the microwave oven was developed from World War II radar technology. Microwaves make water molecules in the food vibrate and this makes the food become hot. Microwave ovens can cook food very quickly.

The invention of the iron cooking range changed cooking dramatically. Among other things it reduced the number of hearth deaths. The Aga cooker is a modern development of the iron range but one which conserves fuel. It was devised in 1924 by a Swedish scientist called Gustav Dalen. The Aga originally ran on solid fuel but is now heated by gas, oil, or electricity.

If food is cooked properly and sealed in a sterile container, it keeps for a very long time. At first, food was preserved in this way in bottles. Tin cans came into use in 1810, to preserve food for soldiers and sailors while they were away on long journeys. However, the food was often badly cooked and contained live bacteria which caused food poisoning. Tins were originally opened using a hammer and chisel. The first openers were developed around 1855, but more sophisticated rotary ones were invented in the 1930s. Nowadays there are electric tin-openers which are especially useful for ill or elderly people.

'Bull's head' tin opener, 1885

▲

Cans of bully beef left by Robert Falcon Scott's Antarctic expedition of 1912 were still edible decades later.

Freezing reduces the activity of the microbes which make food decay. Pre-packed frozen food became popular thanks to the efforts of Clarence Birdseye. He saw how fish caught by Inuit on the Labrador coast froze as soon as they were landed – and were still fresh months later. Birdseye copied the idea when he returned home, patenting a process of fast freezing in 1925. It took a while to become popular, but now people in the US consume nine million tonnes of convenient, hygienic frozen food each year.

Bakelite jug, 1932

▶

Plastic is often used for kitchen surfaces and utensils. It is light and waterproof. However, the first plastics were soft and melted easily. The first tough, heat-resistant plastic was introduced in 1909 by Dr Leo Hendrik Baekeland. He called it 'Bakelite'.

▲

Before washing-up liquid was introduced, people used ashes, sand or brick dust to clean dishes. Scots used heather to scour pots clean.

Nowadays, detergents make washing up a lot easier. Detergents work by reducing the surface tension of water. The oil particles break up and the dirt is held in suspension. The first detergent, called 'Nekal', was made in 1917.

▶

Fingers are very useful for handling food, but they're blunt and they get sticky and dirty. Knives were the first pieces of cutlery to be used, and were a great improvement on human teeth for cutting large chunks of food. The first crude stone knives were made perhaps three million years ago. They were followed much later by spoons and then by forks.

FOOD...

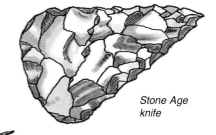

Stone Age knife

Ancient Turkish fork

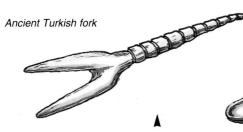

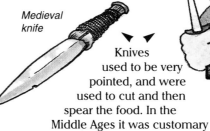

Roman spoon

Some Stone Age wooden forks may date from as long ago as 7000 BC. They were two-pronged which would have made it difficult to skewer small objects. It's thought that they were used to hold down meat while cutting it, in the same way that a carving fork is used nowadays. Modern dining forks originated in Italy, and were brought to England in the seventeenth century by Thomas Coryat.

Medieval knife

Knives used to be very pointed, and were used to cut and then spear the food. In the Middle Ages it was customary to bring your own knife to a meal.

In the Middle Ages, people didn't use plates but instead ate from a large slice of bread or a wooden platter called a trencher. A trencherman is someone who likes to eat a lot of food.

In South Indian food halls, food is served on fresh banana leaves which are cheap, readily available and are thrown away after use.

Chopsticks are used throughout the Far East. They originated in China during the Shang dynasty (c1600–1028 BC). In China, chopsticks were considered superior to knives because they were used by scholars. Scholars were more highly thought of than warriors who carried knives.

Chopsticks can be made from ivory, wood, bamboo, or plastic. As a general rule, the chopsticks of China are longer and more blunt than those of Japan, which are usually tapered. The Japanese tend to use disposable wooden chopsticks, throwing away about twenty billion of them each year.

...AND DRINK

Tea-bags were the idea of an American tea salesman who first tried putting samples of tea into silk bags in the 1920s. Odourless and tasteless paper is now used. The big advantage of tea-bags is that there are no messy leaves to wash out of the teapot.

Many Russians use a samovar for making tea. A central tube is filled with hot charcoal and this tube heats the surrounding water, which brews the tea in a pot on top. The teapot is refilled from the hot water.

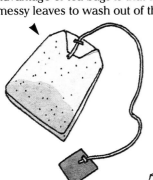

Aluminium is not normally used for teapots because it turns the tea black.

In seventeenth-century England, people would pour their tea from the cup into the saucer to cool it before drinking it. This practice changed gradually and the saucer now goes under the cup to catch spilt liquid. Drinking from the saucer is thought to be rude.

Straws have been used since very ancient times when the hollow stems of plants were used. From the late nineteenth century, straws were made from waxed paper, but they are now usually made from plastic.

Corkscrews are used for pulling corks from bottles without breaking up the cork. The earliest descriptions date from Tudor times, but the Reverend Samuel Henshaw devised the easy-to-use, double-thread corkscrew in 1795.

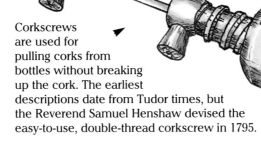

Drinking chocolate was originally a bitter drink made from cocoa beans and spices sacred to the Aztecs of Mexico. They called it *chocolatl*. The court of Montezuma II, the Aztec emperor, is said to have drunk fifty jars a day! The *conquistador* Hernan Cortés introduced cocoa beans to Europe in the 1520s, where the drink later became a popular addition to coffee-house menus as an aid to sleep and digestion. Cocoa beans are now more often used to produce solid chocolate bars and sweets.

Cocoa beans

Clay cart

Wooden dolls' house

TOYS...

All over the world children play with toys and games. Play teaches us to use our imaginations, think logically and move quickly. As in life, there are rules to follow, and penalties to be paid by those who don't.

Pottery donkey

Chalk snobs

Wooden diabolo

Bone flute

Most early toys were made from clay, bone, metal and wood.

Early dolls made from wood, wax, china and rags.

Teddy bears were invented when President Theodore 'Teddie' Roosevelt refused to kill a bear cub when out hunting. In 1902 a sweet shop owner called Morris Michtom saw a cartoon of this episode in a newspaper, and asked if he could make a small bear and name it 'Teddy's Bear'. Cuddly teddies were soon being produced and sold by the thousand. The early teddy bears looked more like real bears than later versions.

Spinning tops were known in ancient Greece and the Far East. They became popular in Europe in the fourteenth century. By the nineteenth century there were professional top spinners who could make tops jump steps or 'walk' up a slope.

...AND GAMES

Greek marble ▲

Modern glass marble ▲

Early dice were originally fashioned from sheeps' ankle bones and had only four numbered sides. Later, the Romans used dice with

▲

six numbered sides which they called *tesserae. Tesserae* were made of bone, ivory or a stone called onyx. They roll easily but come to rest with one face clearly facing upwards so that they can be used to determine results in games of chance.

Marbles were played by Ancient Greeks, Romans and Egyptians. In Greece real marble spheres were used. The game of marbles is a child's version of bowls, and in some parts of Scotland the game is still called 'bools'.

The earliest chess pieces may date from the second century AD. Known as the war game *chaturanga,* chess was certainly played in seventh-century India. *Chaturanga* had four types of piece including the horse which developed into the knight, and the chariot which became the castle. ▶

Twelfth-century chess knight

Some Tarot cards

The first playing cards used in Europe were a set of twenty-two, called the Tarot. The Tarot were picture cards. Gambling games could be played with them, and they were also used for fortune telling. They were combined with a set of fifty-six suited and numbered cards, which arrived in Europe from the East around AD 1300, to create a pack of seventy-eight cards. Later, the French reduced the number to fifty-two, and the Tarot split off to be used purely for fortune telling.

◀

◀

A seventeenth-century French playing card

◁ Ching, Chang, Pok! ▷

Here's a game you can play without any special equipment – the ancient Eastern game known as Ching, Chang, Pok. At the count of three, two players hold out one hand each and make a symbol at the same time. The skill is deciding what hand-symbol your opponent will show next. There is no score if both players show the same symbol. Keep playing until one player reaches an agreed number of wins.

Stone breaks scissors (stone wins)

Scissors cut paper (scissors win)

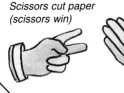
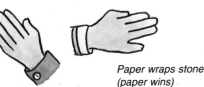

Paper wraps stone (paper wins)

◀

Casinos use fixed-value gaming chips on roulette tables. This avoids handling lots of cash, giving change and checking for forgeries.

73

ON THE STREET

City streets are full of signs, lights and other constructions. All these things are called street furniture. They all have, or have had, a purpose.

Road surface — Side view of cat's-eye

Rubber case — Glass reflectors — Flexible rubber pad

Cat's-eyes were patented by Percy Shaw in 1934. They consist of a prism reflector mounted in a rubber pad. The prism reflects the light from car headlights. They were especially useful during World War II when there was a blackout in Britain and cars travelled with dimmed headlights so that enemy bombers could not see them.

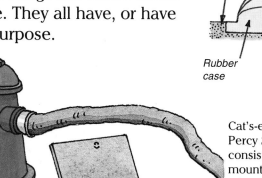

Fire hydrants and standpipes supply water for fighting fires. In America fire hydrants are above ground and are painted red to be easily seen. English hydrants are under the street surface. Signs direct fire-fighters towards the nearest hydrant.

When cars were scarce, people could park anywhere – as they do today in small villages. But as cars multiplied it became necessary to control where they parked, and local councils saw an opportunity to make money. Parking meters originated in the USA, invented in 1932 by Carlton C Magee.

Public telephones came into use in 1922.

British telephone box, 1936

Manhole covers are iron or steel inspection hatches for gas, electricity, telephone, water and sewerage utilities. The covers are rough to prevent people slipping on them, and they are lifted using a special key. You can often read the name of the maker and even the date on them. Sometimes a sign is placed on a wall opposite a manhole cover as a guide to its position.

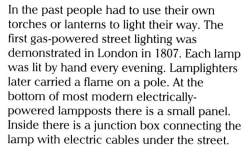

In the past people had to use their own torches or lanterns to light their way. The first gas-powered street lighting was demonstrated in London in 1807. Each lamp was lit by hand every evening. Lamplighters later carried a flame on a pole. At the bottom of most modern electrically-powered lampposts there is a small panel. Inside there is a junction box connecting the lamp with electric cables under the street.

French street toilet

There have been public lavatories since ancient times. Until private lavatories started to be installed in houses, most ordinary households used communal neighbourhood lavatories. In the nineteenth century, sewerage systems were introduced for public health reasons. It cost a penny to use public conveniences in Britain, and many people still 'spend a penny' even in their own homes.

Drains were used in India (2500 BC) and Crete (1500 BC) to carry away rainwater and sewage. Without drains, rainwater causes temporary flooding. Since bicycles became widely used, the metal gratings across drain covers have usually been placed at right-angles to the street, so that narrow wheels don't get stuck in them.

J P Knight, a British railway signalling engineer, invented a system of red and green gas lights with semaphore arms to direct horse-drawn traffic outside the Houses of Parliament. They were installed around 1868. Unfortunately a light exploded and killed the policeman operating it.

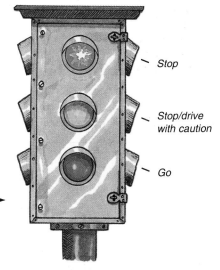

Stop

Stop/drive with caution

Go

The first electric traffic lights were set up in Cleveland, Ohio in 1914. They had only red and green lights. The three-colour system was introduced in New York in 1918, where it was operated by hand from a 'crow's nest' in the middle of the street. The first automatic traffic lights followed, in London, in 1925.

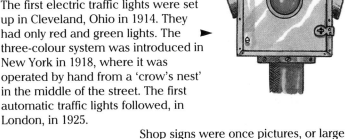

Modern direction signs are written in large letters so that drivers can read them as they approach them. Old signposts pointed towards the next town and could only be read as a vehicle passed, which meant that drivers had to slow down in order to read them. Life without signs would be very inconvenient. During World War II, signposts in Britain were removed to confuse possible enemy invaders.

Shop signs were once pictures, or large models of objects, rather than names because most people could not read.

Tailor

Pawnbroker

Chemist

Money is a means of exchange between merchants or customers which is more convenient than bartering. The Lydians of Asia Minor are said to have introduced metal coinage around 700 BC. Paper money was invented by the Chinese around fourteen hundred years ago.

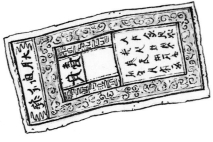

On Pacific islands people used cowrie shells as money.

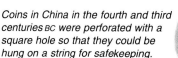

Lydian coin

Coins in China in the fourth and third centuries BC were perforated with a square hole so that they could be hung on a string for safekeeping.

Hard slabs of compressed tea were used as currency in Tibet.

GONE SHOPPING

Shops are as old as civilization. Even in ancient times they had an open front to display the goods, and perhaps a counter. Shop-keepers would often work in their shops manufacturing goods to sell. 'Shop' originally meant 'workshop'. Early shops specialized in one or two commodities and whole streets would be given up to a particular trade. There is evidence of this in most old towns from street names such as 'Butcher Row' or 'Smith Street'.

The cash register was invented in Ohio, USA, in 1879 by James Ritty. Cash registers record sales, add up prices and protect money already collected. Modern versions can read bar codes which give information directly to the till without any need to type it in.

Old cash register

Some bank-notes contain a silver security strip; this and other features make bank-notes difficult to forge.

The writer A P Herbert once presented a cheque written on a cow!

In Britain, a legal cheque can be written on anything. A cheque is an instruction to your bank to pay money to someone from your account. Cheques and credit cards are more secure and convenient than carrying around large amounts of cash.

A unique serial number on each half of the note

Complicated pictures, with lots of tiny lines which are hard to copy

Specially made paper, with areas made extra thin, called watermarks

A short history of one-stop shopping

Shopping malls, or shopping centres, combine many shops under one roof. The first 'shopping mall' was built by Sir Thomas Gresham in London in 1568.

Department stores sell many different types of goods under one roof. The first department store was built in Paris in 1850.

Supermarkets are self service stores that sell a wide range of groceries. The first supermarket was opened by Michael Cullen in 1930 in Jamaica, New York.

Not everyone likes shopping. It's time-consuming and hard work if you have to visit a lot of different shops to find the things you need. Putting different shops under one roof is a great help – but getting the shopping home has always been a problem.

Price labels were first widely used in the eighteenth century to avoid haggling. Aristocratic French refugees who fled to England after the French Revolution were amazed to see that even wandering butchers and grocers would stick labels on all the various goods on their trays. In addition to price tags, shops now fix security tags to packages to make it more difficult to steal them.

Old shopping trolley

Shopping baskets on wheels (shopping trolleys) were introduced in 1936 by S N Goldman of Standard Humpty Dumpty Food Markets. His business boomed as people piled goods onto their trolleys knowing that they would not have to carry heavy bags around the store.

Handling sugar too much causes a skin disease called 'grocer's itch'.

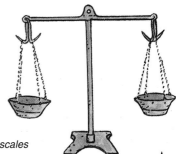

Roman scales

In many countries, goods may be wrapped by the shopkeeper in plain paper or even in large leaves. Pre-packaging is a recent development that keeps goods fresh and clean, saves time in the shop and allows the producer to describe and advertise the product, but also produces a lot of waste.

Weighing is often the easiest way to assess the volume or quantity of goods, and weighing scales have been used for thousands of years. Modern electronic scales are very accurate. Goods can be weighed, and the price and weight are automatically registered at the till.

SCHOOL GEAR

Children have been going to school for thousands of years, and it's never been very popular with them. But the schools of today are very different from those of the past and so are the things that are used in the classroom.

For centuries children sent to boarding school have used large school trunks. They might stay at school right through each term so they needed plenty of clothes and other items. ▶

The blackboard came into existence in the early nineteenth century when a Scottish teacher had the idea of writing on a black painted board with a white chalk. To make coloured chalk he mixed ground chalk with colouring and used porridge to bind them together.

▲ Old fashioned desks had lift-up lids for storing equipment and books inside them, and ink wells into which pens were dipped. The seat was often fixed to the desk, or there might be several desks fixed together with a bench seat.

The whiteboard is a recent development. Special marker pens are used on a white surface. The board is cleaned with a damp cloth so there's no chalk dust, and no more banging out chalky board rubbers against the edge of a blackboard. ▶

Felt marker pen

78

Paper has only recently become cheap enough to use in large quantities in the classroom. For hundreds of years, children used slates to write on instead of paper. Slates can be re-used by rubbing out the previous work. They are still used in some countries round the world.

Roman and Medieval children used wax tablets, made with a layer of wax on a wooden base. Writing was done with a stylus – a stick of reed or metal, sharp at one end for writing and flat at the other end so that the wax could be smoothed out and re-used.

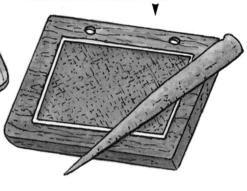

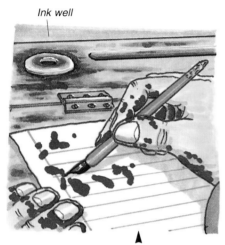

Ink well

Dip-pens were used in schools until the 1960s. They leaked, and many schoolchildren had blue, inky fingers for most of the time.

'Lead' pencil

Early pencils were made from a piece of lead encased in wood. In 1795 Nicholas-Jacques Conté produced pencils made from graphite which had been ground, formed into sticks and baked in a kiln. The graphite in pencils is still called 'lead'.

Eraser

The first rubber erasers were sold in 1770 by an English maker of mathematical instruments called Mr Nairne. They were called rubbers because they can rub out pencil marks – the material we call rubber is named after rubbers, and not the other way round! Natural rubber is a milky liquid, tapped from trees, which hardens in the open air. A similar material produced from dandelions was used during the British rubber shortage in World War II.

Modern fountain pen

Joseph Bramah patented the fountain-pen in 1809. It allowed people to write without constantly having to dip their pens in a bottle of ink. Unfortunately, the stodgy ink kept blocking up the pen.

In 1884, a capillary feed mechanism was developed by Lewis E Waterman. A lever mechanism sucked smooth ink into a rubber sac. Nowadays many ink pens contain a plastic ink cartridge which can be replaced when empty.

The first ball-point pen was invented by the American John Loud, in 1888. An improved version was invented in 1938 by two Hungarian brothers – Lazlo and Georg Biro. The ball at the point of the pen rotates, bringing the ink from the tube to the paper. A special formula ink was later developed by Franz Seech which dried instantly on contact with air, preventing smudges. Biros could write under water and they did not leak at high altitudes or low atmospheric pressures. Biros became the standard pens issued to soldiers of the US Army during World War II.

The Biro ballpoint pen

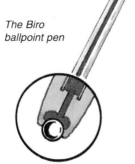

GARDENING GADGETS

People were originally gatherers of wild fruits, cereals and vegetables. Later they became skilled at cultivating their own plants, and became farmers. At a very early date, plants were no doubt planted with an eye to their beauty as well as their food value. One of the Seven Wonders of the ancient world was the Hanging Gardens of Babylon. Built by King Nebuchadnezzar II in about 600 BC in honour of his Queen, Amyitis, the gardens of trees, vines, shrubs, and flowers were planted on a huge stepped pyramid fifty metres high. ►

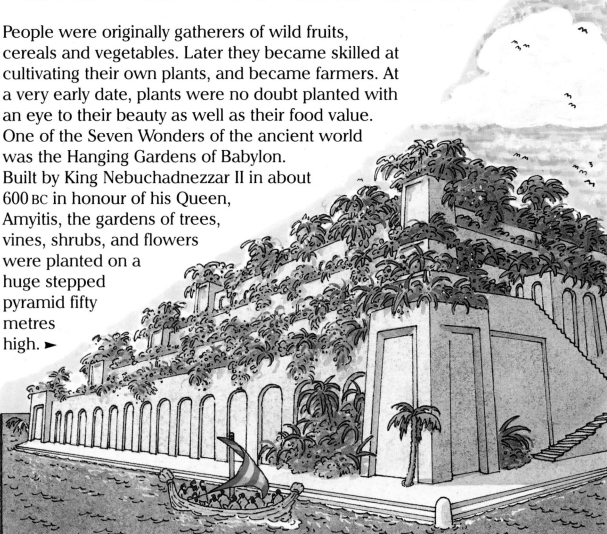

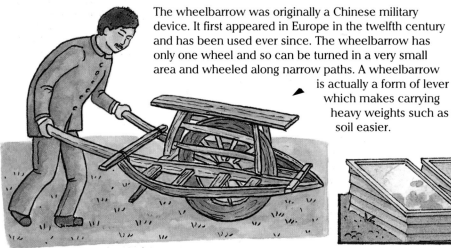

The wheelbarrow was originally a Chinese military device. It first appeared in Europe in the twelfth century and has been used ever since. The wheelbarrow has only one wheel and so can be turned in a very small area and wheeled along narrow paths. A wheelbarrow is actually a form of lever which makes carrying heavy weights such as soil easier.

The cold frame was probably a sixteenth-century Dutch invention and was used to protect young plants and make them grow quickly without artificial heating. 'Cold frames' are actually 'warm frames'!

The lawn as we know it is an English invention dating from the early eighteenth century. Scythes and shears were used to cut the grass, but they could not cut it very short. Lawns with short grass were not a practical proposition until the first cylinder mower was patented by Edwin Budding in 1830. He got the idea from a factory machine which trimmed the pile on cloth. The first large models were pulled by a pony or horse wearing special leather shoes to prevent the animal's hooves from damaging the turf.

Early spades were made of wood strengthened with an iron tip. Later the heads were made of iron or steel for greater strength.

French peasants often used a spade without a handle.

Edwin Budding's lawn mower

The first steam-driven mowers appeared in 1893, followed by petrol mowers at the beginning of the twentieth century.

Simple hand-mower

The fork is useful for breaking up the soil and for digging up root vegetables without damaging them.

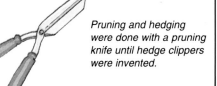

The Flymo was introduced in 1963. It is based on the hovercraft principle. The mower is supported on a cushion of air created by an electric fan so that it can be pulled or pushed in any direction.

Pruning and hedging were done with a pruning knife until hedge clippers were invented.

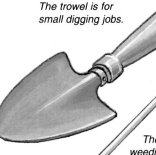

The trowel is for small digging jobs.

Most plants need watering in dry weather or they will die. Originally, watering was done by hand from a can. This meant that in dry weather big gardens needed large numbers of gardeners to do the watering. The first hoses appeared in 1850. They were made from gutta-percha, a kind of rubber. Hoses enabled large areas of garden to be watered quite easily.

The hoe is for weeding. The sharp blade cuts the roots of the weeds. The loose soil passes through the hole as the hoe is turned.

In 1968 Kress and Kestner of the German company Gardena produced hoses with plastic components which simply clicked together.

The digging stick is an African tool used for breaking up hard-packed soil.

The dibber makes holes for seeds and small plants.

Many sports developed from real fighting techniques...

Archery bows evolved from medieval long-bows.

Fencing is a bloodless form of sword fighting.

Javelins are standardized spears.

SPORT

Some sports have a very ancient origin, and so does some sports equipment. Balls were used in sport by the Ancient Egyptians, and were probably made of blown-up pigs' bladders or other inflated parts of an animal. Bladders were used in footballs until quite recently when modern materials were developed.

The dimensions of a soccer ball were first set by the Football ▲ Association in the nineteenth century. Until recently footballs were made of leather, becoming very heavy and water-logged on a muddy pitch. The modern plastic coating keeps them dry.

Cutaway showing inflatable bladder

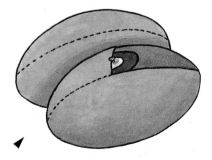

◄

The balls used in American football and Rugby football are egg-shaped so that they can be thrown accurately. This shape also makes it difficult to dribble the ball along the ground.

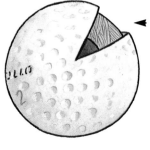

◄ A golf ball is covered in tiny dimples. Air flowing past these dimples helps to make the ball fly further and straighter than if it were smooth. Seventeenth-century golf balls were filled with feathers but now contain a variety of synthetic elastic materials.

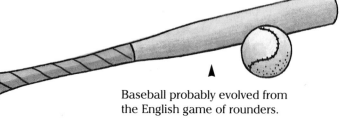

▲

Baseball probably evolved from the English game of rounders.

82

Polo, which is rather like hockey on horseback, developed as a training for war. The game may have been invented by the Persians in the first century AD. Polo sticks have a long flexible haft and are quite light so that they can be wielded with one hand.

Buzkashi is a game like polo, played in Afghanistan. Games may involve a thousand horsemen. Instead of a ball, players throw or bash the body of a goat around to score goals. In one version a flat goat is used...

Croquet probably developed from the French game of *paille-maille* in the Middle Ages. Balls are hit between hoops on a lawn. The haft of a croquet mallet is shorter than a polo stick and the head is heavier.

...and in another version the goat is inflated.

The name of cricket may come from its bat, or perhaps from its wicket: *creag'et* is Anglo-Saxon for a staff or stick. Nowadays the hitting part of the bat is made from willow which is a very springy wood. Interestingly, the length of a cricket pitch is about the width of a Saxon strip field.

Kites probably originated in China around 1000 BC. Some were large enough to carry a man and were used for war. In Japan and Thailand, kite-fighting between large 'male' kites and smaller but more agile 'female' ones is very popular. Kite strings coated in ground glass or broken porcelain are used to cut the opponent's line.

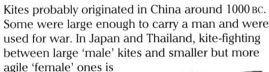

Lacrosse is a Native American game, originally called *baggataway*. It was played with as many as a thousand players. Players fought to carry the ball with small nets mounted on wooden sticks. It was a very violent and bloody game often played by more than two sets of opponents at a time.

83

GETTING COMFY

Many early civilizations had no furniture to speak of, and very few home comforts of any kind. Nowadays, the homes of tribal peoples are still often simple, but home has become a place of increasing luxury and comfort for people in many areas. Fixtures like carpets and central heating or cooling systems are now standard.

Carpets were known in Persia in the fifth century BC. They were one of the luxuries brought back to Europe by the Crusaders, who had seen them spread out on the sand in the tents of desert tribesmen as well as on the floors of rich Arab homes. They were a luxury item in Europe until modern production techniques made them cheaper. Even large expanses of fitted carpet are now common. They help to insulate houses as well as providing comfortable floors.

People in Medieval Europe used rushes or straw as floor coverings. It was once illegal in England to throw away rushes which, because they soaked up urine and other wastes, could be used to make gunpowder. The urine provided saltpetre and the rushes provided sulphur and carbon. ►

In the Middle East, cushions and simple mattresses are still used instead of furniture in traditional homes.

In the Middle Ages most people had to make do with stools and benches. Chairs with backs were for important people. So little furniture was available that kings would carry it with them from palace to palace. This was still the custom in the sixteenth century. ▶

Steamed furniture appeared around 1850. Wood is heated in a steam-box until it becomes flexible, then it's bent and clamped. When dried it retains its new shape. ▼

American rocking chair, 1876

▲ Until the sixteenth century, the only form of soft padding was cushions scattered on wooden furniture. Later, horse hair padding, covered in carpet material or velvet, was attached to some expensive furniture. Internal springs were only added in the 1920s.

People in India traditionally relied on small windows and thick walls to keep out the heat of the Sun, or on devices such as tatties. Tatties are mats made of the roots of cuscus grass which are soaked with water and hung outside windows. The room is cooled as the water evaporates. ▼

Indian house with tatties

To clean a dusty silk carpet in the desert it is turned over and the dust and dirt are shaken into the sand by people treading on the other side. ▶

Air-conditioning makes houses a lot more comfortable in warm, moist climates. The idea started in America where Mr Willis H Carrier experimented by passing air through an evaporation chamber. ▼

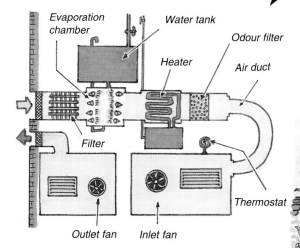

Evaporation chamber

Water tank

Odour filter

Heater

Air duct

Filter

Thermostat

Outlet fan

Inlet fan

Simplified air-conditioning unit

With a central heating system, one fire heats many rooms. This gives an even, comfortable warmth and means fewer fires or boilers to tend. The Romans had under-floor central heating systems known as hypocausts. ▼

Roman hypocaust

HOME ENTERTAINMENT

In the days before television, many people were able to play musical instruments. Standing beside the River Thames at the time of the Great Fire of London in 1666, Samuel Pepys noted that one refugee boat in three had a pair of virginals in it. A virginal was a popular instrument like a small piano. ▶

In the past, people made their own entertainment by playing games or making music, or they told stories about wars and romances, or the adventures of gods and legendary heroes. Home entertainment has changed a lot since then. With the invention of electronic entertainment systems, there are still plenty of games to play and music to make, but nowadays, people watch more and do less.

The first TV picture ever transmitted

The first public demonstration of television was made in 1926 by John Logie Baird. In early transmissions people saw the picture without sound and then the sound without the picture. It was not possible to broadcast sound and pictures at the same time.

Germany transmitted the first regular, filmed TV service in 1935. The broadcast of the Olympic games in 1936 is said to be the first television show with a signal powerful enough to leave the Earth's atmosphere.

The first colour TV transmissions were made in 1940 by the Columbia Broadcasting System (CBS).

In the past people tended to go to bed quite soon after darkness fell. When home lighting improved in the nineteenth century, this change, together with cheaper books and with the start of public libraries, helped to make reading a very popular activity.

Movie camera, 1920

History used to be recorded only by books and story-tellers. These days history is more often recorded on film or video.

Radio, 1930

Radio was originally called 'wireless' because it needed no wires to carry messages, unlike the telephone or telegraph. We still use radios because we can listen whilst doing something else.

Record record

Thomas Alva Edison built the first phonograph in 1877. The first recording was the nursery rhyme 'Mary had a little lamb', made on a tin-foil cylinder.

Emile Berliner demonstrated the first flat record disc in 1888.

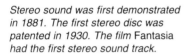

Stereo sound was first demonstrated in 1881. The first stereo disc was patented in 1930. The film Fantasia had the first stereo sound track.

Compact discs were introduced in the 1980s. CDs are popular because they are more hard-wearing than earlier vinyl records.

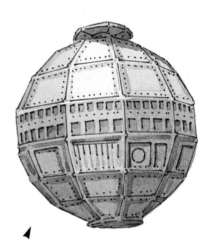

Artificial satellites reflect radio and television signals around the world. The first commercial communications satellite was called *Telstar*, it was launched in 1962.

The coronation of Queen Elizabeth II in 1953 was the first major international broadcast. It was seen in France, West Germany and the Netherlands.

Video recorders were introduced in 1956 by the Ampex company. These huge machines processed 16 km of tape per hour.

The first flat screen display was developed by Matsushita in 1979. In the future, wafer-thin televisions may be hung on a wall.

Shetland Islanders used oily seabirds called storm petrels to light their way. With a wick down their throats, these dead birds made excellent lamps.

During World War I, soldiers burned oil in sardine tins for light.

Native Americans used a dead oily 'candle fish' inserted in a cleft stick as a lamp.

LIGHTING-UP TIME

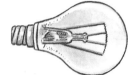

Nowadays, it's so easy to flick a switch and light up a room that it's hard to imagine what life was like before electric light was invented. People used candles and lamps, but the light was very dim so they went to bed early and got up early. In the sixteenth century, a curfew starting at nine o'clock in the evening was normal in many towns. During the curfew everyone had to be indoors. The working day might start at four o'clock the next morning.

Tudor watchman

Limelight was used to light theatre stages from the eighteenth to the late nineteenth centuries. If lime (calcium oxide) is heated to a very high temperature it glows brilliantly white. At first the lime was heated by gas, then later by electrically-powered carbon arcs.

Sir Humphrey Davy invented the electric arc lamp in 1808 but this invention had to wait for suitable electric generators before it could be used for street-lighting. The light it produces is so strong that it cannot be used for domestic lighting. Instead people use arc lamps for floodlighting, large film projectors and for searchlights.

◀ The first practical electric light bulb was devised by Thomas Alva Edison in 1879. Instead of the modern tungsten filament, Edison used a scorched cotton thread.

Whales used to be a major source of lamp oil.

Olive oil has been used in southern Europe since at least the time of the Ancient Greeks.

The first oil well, Titusville, Pennsylvania

The first oil well was sunk in 1859. Soon paraffin was being distilled from crude oil and paraffin lamps became very popular. They were much brighter than previous lamps or candles, though they still used a wick.

For most of history the majority of poor families in Europe used reed lamps. Fuel for reed lamps was melted down fat from meat, called tallow. The tallow would seep up a reed wick planted in it. When the tip of the reed was lit, the tallow burned slowly, giving light and a slight smell of food. Reed lamps are no longer used because of the smell, the poor light and the bother of making tallow and wicks.

The Chinese were the first to use gas light. There are early Chinese references to bamboo pipes being filled with marsh gas (methane).

In a Tilly lamp, paraffin vapour burns brightly as it passes through a fine net structure called a mantle.

The fluorescent light is a glass tube coated on the inside with chemicals which glow, or fluoresce, when electricity is passed through a gas within the tube. Unlike other electric lights, fluorescent strips do not get hot and they give a bright economical light. Fluorescent lighting became known to the general public after the New York World Fair in 1939.

Davy lamps were invented by Sir Humphrey Davy in 1815. A very explosive gas called methane, or fire damp, builds up in mines. It caused many disasters when lit by the naked candle flames carried by early miners. In Davy's lamp the flame is covered by a wire gauze with 120 holes per square centimetre, so methane cannot get through the gauze in enough quantity to explode. Instead, the flame becomes brighter when methane is present, warning the miner of possible danger.

Good candles were often more expensive than oil lamps. They were originally made from tallow and so were rather smelly, but were later made from beeswax or paraffin wax. They are still widely used because some people consider harsh electric light to be less attractive.

The wick on a candle has to be plaited so that it falls sideways and does not put out the flame.

WINDOWS

The trouble with houses is that if they have no holes in their walls they are dark, and if they do have holes in their walls they are either draughty or too hot. Windows help to solve this problem. A window is a hole in the wall, usually with a piece of transparent material placed across it, so that light can enter, but wind and rain are kept out.

Houses in hot countries have small windows to reduce the flow of hot air into the cool, shady interior.

In cooler countries, where light is needed but not the cold wind, small windows are built in the walls of houses where the coldest winds blow. Larger windows are built in the opposite walls to catch the heat of the Sun.

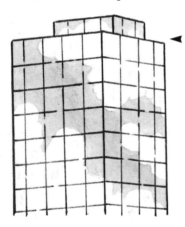

Outer skins of large, modern buildings are often 'glass curtains' which may be tinted to reflect the Sun's heat. Recently, glass with a special clear coating has been developed which lets in light and heat but prevents heat from leaving. This is useful for saving heating energy in cold countries.

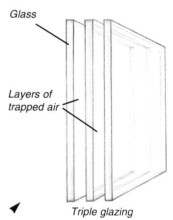

Glass

Layers of trapped air

Triple glazing

Air is a poor conductor of heat. A layer of air trapped between two sheets of glass reduces the amount of heat lost from a building, and also reduces noise. In some cold places like Norway and Sweden triple glazing is built into all new homes.

In the Arabian desert, the Bedu tribespeople roll up the sides of their tents to let in light and air.

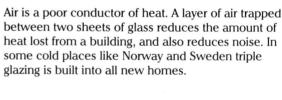

Glass actually acts like a very thick liquid. Over the years, glass sheets flow downwards so that they are thicker at the bottom than the top.

Japanese houses traditionally have no glass windows, possibly because Japan is in an earthquake zone. Instead sliding doors are covered with rice paper which allows light to filter in.

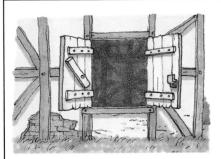

Windows must provide security against intruders. The earliest windows were holes which could be closed with shutters.

The Romans used glass in their windows but they could not produce large, flat, clear pieces. Their glass windows were very small.

In the Middle Ages windows were often covered with a thin layer of horn, oil-cloth or waxed paper. Wooden shutters with decorative holes were also used.

In the fourteenth century, glass was spun from a large disc of molten glass which was flat around the edges but ridged like the bottom of a glass bottle in the centre. Flat thick 'crown' glass was cut from the edges, leaving 'bottle' glass in the centre which was either recycled or used by someone who did not mind the distortion.

In Tudor cottages small diamonds of crown glass were joined together by lead strips. By 1918 larger pieces of plate glass were made by grinding and smoothing flat ribbons of molten glass drawn from a heating vat.

Float glass was introduced in 1952. Sheets of molten glass are floated on molten tin. The tin is smooth and flat, and glass does not stick to it. When the glass is cool enough and smooth on both sides it's taken off on rollers.

Sash windows slide up and down. The moving parts are balanced by counterweights set in the frame on each side of the window to make opening and closing the window easy. They were first used in the seventeenth century.

A casement window is hinged on one side and has a latch to hold it open or closed. Most casement windows have side hinges.

Roller blinds are space-saving, instant coverings for windows.

Venetian blinds are vertical or horizontal slats of wood, metal or plastic which can be adjusted to allow in varying amounts of light.

Net curtains make it difficult for passers-by to see into houses during daylight hours.

ALL LOCKED UP

The design of both doors and locks has changed over the centuries, but not the reason why we need them. In some cases even the design remains the same – there is a lock in use in Egypt today based on a design which may be over three thousand years old.

Janus was the Roman god of doorways and of beginnings and endings. He had two faces and could look both forwards and backwards at the same time.

Roman coin showing Janus

The Romans had folding doors which moved on pivots fixed into the sill and the lintel.

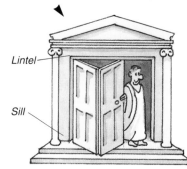

Lintel

Sill

This door hinge, first patented in 1799, lifts the door over the edge of a rug. ▶

The earliest examples of metal hinges are made of copper and were found on treasure chests in the tomb of the Pharaoh Tutankhamen (1357-1338 BC).

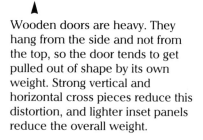

Wooden doors are heavy. They hang from the side and not from the top, so the door tends to get pulled out of shape by its own weight. Strong vertical and horizontal cross pieces reduce this distortion, and lighter inset panels reduce the overall weight.

Knobs and latches

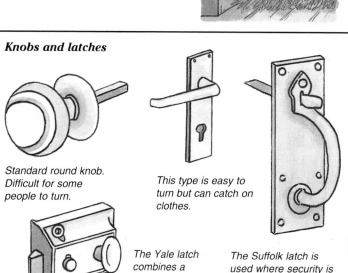

Standard round knob. Difficult for some people to turn.

This type is easy to turn but can catch on clothes.

The Yale latch combines a lock with a doorknob.

The Suffolk latch is used where security is unnecessary.

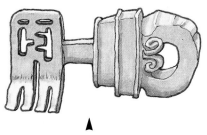

Roman iron key

The first locks and keys were wooden and were probably invented by the Chinese about 4,500 years ago. The Romans developed complex iron and bronze locks.

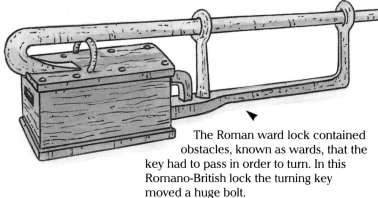

The Roman ward lock contained obstacles, known as wards, that the key had to pass in order to turn. In this Romano-British lock the turning key moved a huge bolt.

Metal padlocks were first produced in Nuremberg in the 1540s, where they were used for locking boxes.

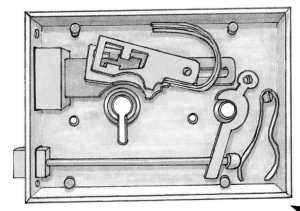

Edwardian mortise lock

In 1778 an English locksmith called Robert Barron together with Joseph Bramah (see below) made the forerunner to the mortise lock. These use levers that must be moved to an exact distance by the key before the bolt can be moved.

For most of history, people have kept their valuables in large heavy chests or strong boxes. The first secure, fireproof safe was introduced by Thomas Milner and Charles Chubb in 1845.

Joseph Bramah patented the first barrel lock in 1784. His key had slits and notches which depressed sprung segments in a cylinder to different depths. At the correct depth the groove on the edge of all the segments lined up and the entire barrel could be revolved by the key to draw the bolt. Bramah was so confident of the security of his invention that he offered 200 guineas to anyone who could pick it. Sixty-seven years later, at the Great Exhibition of 1851 an American locksmith called Alfred Hobbs succeeded, but only after hours of laborious effort.

Most bank safes have a time lock so that the safe can only be opened at certain times.

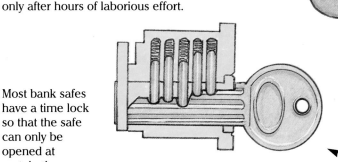

The Yale lock patented in 1865 by the American, Linus Yale Jr, has been the most successful lock of all time. The five wards have an almost infinite variety of positions, so it is very secure.

93

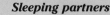

Cats often prefer a big comfy bed to a cat basket.

The bed bug drinks human blood. It can take in up to seven times its own body volume of blood during a feeding session.

Fleas suck blood too.

An average mattress contains large quantities of dead skin and old sweat. These provide a wonderful supply of delicious food and drink for bed mites.

AND SO TO BED...

We spend about a third of our lives in bed so it's important to be comfortable and warm. In the past, people often shared their beds with the rest of the family, especially on cold nights. Even farm animals sometimes slept in the same room!

Headboards prevent pillows from falling off the end of the bed. Footboards prevent bedclothes falling off the other end.

The Celestial Bed was invented by Dr James Graham in about 1778. It was surrounded by 762 kg of magnets which he claimed were good for the health. There was a charge of 500 guineas a night to sleep in it.

▲ The Indian charpoy is a simple wooden bedstead with netting for support.

▲ South Americans Indians and Caribs slept in hammocks made of woven material. The idea was adopted by Europeans for their ships because hammocks allow sleeping sailors to remain undisturbed by the rolling of the ship.

High-sided bunk-beds on ships helped to prevent passengers and sailors falling out of bed during stormy weather.

◀ The Japanese futon is a slatted wooden bed which is usually covered with a cotton-padded mattress.

Camp-beds were first used by ▲ soldiers when on campaign. Officers took collapsible beds with them. Tutankhamen used a fold-up bed when travelling around his kingdom.

KNOW-IT-ALL NED'S

You've probably met smarty-pants people who think they are always right – but hardly ever are! Take Know-it-all Ned for example. Most of what he's saying is rubbish! Can you tell when he's right and when he's wrong?...

QUIZ

WHY DO WE?

"...the baseball bat is rounded because early baseball grew out of a game in which the round handle of a cricket bat was used to hit a ball..."

"Samovars are special teapots named after an Irish explorer who introduced tea into Europe in 1536..."

"...some Indians hang up wet grass to cool their houses..."

"...Roman generals used strops to protect their feet against hypocausts..."

"...modern 'fountain' pens were invented by Mr Waterman in 1884..."

"...medieval monks recycled scrolls for toilet paper..."

"...'ward locks' are so named because they help to prevent burglaries in hospitals..."

"...'light' olive oil was used in lamps by Ancient Albanians..."

"...dried cow-pats are used for cooking food in some countries in Asia and Africa."

"...'float' glass is called this after the process by which it is made..."

"...frozen fish was first eaten by a shipwrecked sailor, Finlay Codburger, in 1868..."

"...in the game of Ching, Chang, Pok, 'runny noses' can be covered by 'hankies'..."

ANSWERS:

1: Wrong	2: Wrong	3: Right
4: Wrong	5: Right	6: Wrong
7: Wrong	8: Right	9: Right
10: Wrong	11: Right	12: Wrong

95

WHY DO WE CELEBRATE THAT?

Being born is the first big event in anyone's life, even though the baby is too young to know what is going on. Parents often want to give thanks for a new child, and its safe birth. Religious ceremonies and traditional customs help introduce children to the duties and beliefs of the society into which they are born.

BEING BORN

The Spartans of ancient Greece believed that babies were government property. Babies had to be strong enough to grow up to be warriors or healthy wives. Elders of the city inspected the new-born and ordered weak-looking babies to be placed outside the city to die.

Muslims believe that a baby should be introduced to Islam very soon after it is born. At the Tahneek ceremony, a sweet is placed in the child's mouth to make the child kind and obedient. At the Ageegah ceremony, the baby's head is shaved and the baby is named. The cut hair is weighed and its weight in silver is given to charity or to the poor. Then a sheep or goat is sacrificed (two for a boy, one for a girl), cooked and shared.

Christening

In the West, people are often christened in church when they are quite young. The service is a reminder of the baptism of Jesus in the River Jordan by John the Baptist.

At the christening, parents and chosen godparents undertake to bring up the child as a Christian. Holy water from the font is sprinkled three times on the baby's head, for each member of the Trinity: God the Father, the Son and the Holy Spirit. A sign of the cross is made on the child's head with water.

Some Australian tribes used to knock out the two front teeth of their babies. Legend says that this was done by the good spirit, Muramura, to his own children, and the Australians carried on the tradition to please the tribal spirits.

▼

Jewish and Muslim boys are circumcised soon after birth, meaning a piece is cut from the penis foreskin. This is done by the Jews as a sign of their covenant, or agreement, with God.

The umbilical cord carries food and oxygen from the mother to the unborn child. This cord is sacred to some Buddhists, who preserve it in salt and bury it in a pot under two coconut trees.

Hindus believe in karma – that people are rewarded or punished for the things they do during their lifetimes. According to Hindu belief, the spirit lives forever, even though the person's body dies. The spirit is reborn in a new body that is either human or animal, depending on how good the person has been in the previous life. For example, someone who has been cruel to birds might be reborn as a bird in the next life.

In the Philippine Islands, there is a tradition that the mother and her new-born baby have to live near a specially built fire for a week. In order to purify the mother, water is poured over rocks heated by the fire.

Many Chinese believe that evil spirits can steal young babies away if they know the child's name. For this reason no name is given to the baby for thirty days. Then a feast is held and the baby is named.

Native Americans traditionally have names that describe some event in their childhood. For example, a member of the tribe might be called Broken Leg or Rides the Grey Mare.

Children are not considered full members of society because they don't know enough, and don't know right from wrong. Most cultures feel a need to celebrate the passage from childhood to adulthood. Ceremonies to mark this 'coming of age' may involve physical pain or insults, or the child might make a vow to follow the society's rules. After this initiation ceremony he or she is usually treated as an adult with new rights and duties.

COMING OF AGE

For a Sikh boy to enter the Khalsa, or community of adults, he must go through a ceremony in a holy place. The Mul Mantra, which sums up Sikh beliefs, is chanted, and the young man drinks, and is sprinkled with, a special sweet concoction called 'amrit'. Members of the Khalsa must wear five special sacred things: the five Ks.

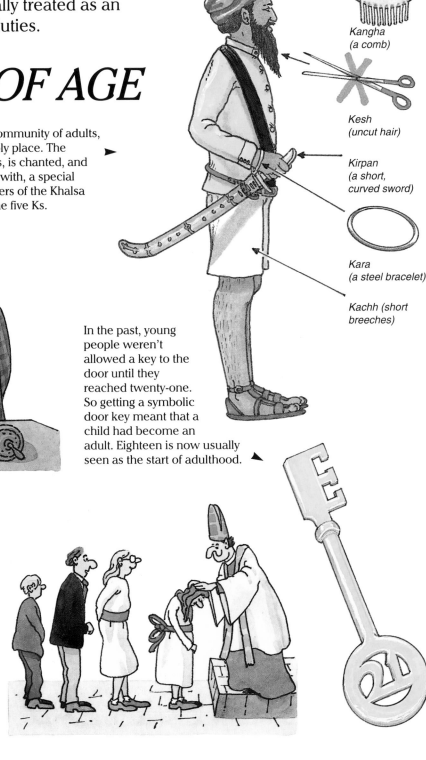

Kangha
(a comb)

Kesh
(uncut hair)

Kirpan
(a short,
curved sword)

Kara
(a steel bracelet)

Kachh (short
breeches)

In the past, young people weren't allowed a key to the door until they reached twenty-one. So getting a symbolic door key meant that a child had become an adult. Eighteen is now usually seen as the start of adulthood. ►

Under Jewish law, once a boy reaches thirteen and a girl twelve, they are able to play an adult role in the life of the community and the synagogue. The ceremonies of Bar Mitzvah (boys) and Bat Mitzvah (girls) celebrate the passage to adulthood.

Most Christian churches hold a service of Confirmation for those in their early teens, when the vows ► made for them at their christening are confirmed. Confirmation is usually carried out by a bishop who places his hand on each child's head as they confirm their beliefs.

100

In East Africa, a Masai boy has to become a warrior as well as an adult. He must be brave enough to face lions and other tribal enemies. The boy's head is shaved, he takes a ritual bath and is then publicly circumcised with a sharp stone. He must not show any sign of pain or fear. After the ceremony, the boys grow their hair and dye it and their clothes with red clay.

Australian Aboriginals traditionally go through a fiery initiation. They either walk through fire or have fire applied to their bodies. ▼

In the Taulipang tribe of South America, a boy is whipped and cut on the chin, arms and feet. A bucket of stinging ants is held to his chest. The whipping is meant to purify him, the cuts make him an expert with the bow or the blow pipe and the ants keep him always alert. If the boy shows any pain, he must go through the ordeal again. ▼

▲ Among Buddhists, there is no coming of age ceremony but it is common for boys between ten and twenty to spend time in a Buddhist monastery. In Burma, the boys re-enact the story of Siddhartha, in which a luxury-loving prince became the Enlightened One.

Zoroastrians, whose faith originated in ancient Persia, have a ceremony called Naojote to initiate young people into their religion. The priest dresses the new member in a white garment ▼ called a 'Sadre' and a thin girdle called a 'Kusti'. The Kusti has seventy-two strands of lamb's wool to represent the seventy-two chapters of their prayer book. As they pray the Kusti is tied around the waist three times, symbolizing good words, good thoughts and good deeds.

WEDDINGS

Marriage is the joining together of a man (the groom) and a woman (the bride) to make a couple who usually intend to stay together for the rest of their lives.

In a traditional Albanian wedding, the groom pretends to capture the bride, then takes her to his home where she has to stand in front of a fire. She has to hold a pair of tongs and cannot speak or sleep for three days. This symbolizes her dutiful promise to her new household. Then the groom gives the bride a leather belt to wear and the couple are considered married.

Before a wedding takes place in England, 'banns' are read in the church for three weeks running. This is so that people will know of the coming marriage, and anyone who knows a reason why the couple should not marry has a chance to object. The bride's costume has three main symbols. White symbolizes purity. The bouquet of flowers symbolizes fertility. The ring goes on the third finger of the left hand because an ancient Greek belief was that a particular vein connected this finger with the heart.

Jewish weddings take place under a chuppah, or canopy, decorated with flowers. After the ceremony, the groom breaks a wine glass underfoot. This is a reminder of the destruction of Jewish temples by the Babylonians and the Romans.

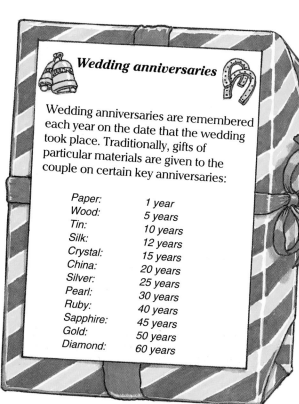

Wedding anniversaries

Wedding anniversaries are remembered each year on the date that the wedding took place. Traditionally, gifts of particular materials are given to the couple on certain key anniversaries:

Paper:	1 year
Wood:	5 years
Tin:	10 years
Silk:	12 years
Crystal:	15 years
China:	20 years
Silver:	25 years
Pearl:	30 years
Ruby:	40 years
Sapphire:	45 years
Gold:	50 years
Diamond:	60 years

In some Native American tribes, it was the custom for a woman to propose marriage. She did this by lighting a fire outside the man's tent and baking a cake. If the man ate the cake, the couple were considered engaged to be married.

Hindu marriages often take place in the house of the bride, who is dressed in red material with gold thread and wears gold jewellery and decorations of henna dye on her hands and feet. The elephant god Ganesha is worshipped by the couple on the day before the wedding.

Chinese weddings begin with an exchange of gifts between the two families and an agreement of the bride price. This sum is compensation to the bride's parents for the cost of bringing up the bride. Horoscopes are read to find out if the couple will be happily married. The ceremony takes place in the groom's house and consists of prayers and offerings to ancestors and the household gods.

The honeymoon is based on the ancient European tradition of drinking honey wine, or mead, for a month after the wedding. Attila the Hun (AD 406–453) is said to have died from drinking too much mead after his wedding.

In many Muslim marriages the man who performs the ceremony writes three copies of the wedding certificate. This is an agreement between the bride and the groom to follow the rules of marriage.

Spring festivals are often celebrations marking the end of winter. The arrival of new plants and the lengthening of the days were very important to early societies.

SPRING

Purim is a celebration of the escape of the Jews from the evil clutches of Haman, the chief minister for the king of Persia, Ahasuerus. Haman wanted all the Jews enslaved or killed, starting with the proud and rebellious Mordecai. He began by building a gallows to hang Mordecai. However, King Ahasuerus was married to Mordecai's niece, Esther. She persuaded the king to have Haman hanged instead – and to make Mordecai the new chief minister. When the story is read to children, they hiss at Haman's name and eat cakes they call 'Haman's purse' or 'Haman's ears'. ▼

▲

Palm Sunday marks the end of Lent (the 40 days before Christ was crucified) and the entry of Christ into Jerusalem. It was then the custom to wave palm branches in honour of holy visitors. Nowadays, processions are held on Palm Sunday around or between churches with palms or crosses made from palm leaves.

Indian dancing is wonderfully expressive and Shivrati is a festival celebrating Shiva, the Lord of the Dance. It is held in the month of Phalguna (February – March). ▼

An Indian devadasi, or temple dancer

Good Friday, originally 'God's Friday', is the day that Jesus was executed on a cross. Hot-cross ► buns are eaten on this day, a tradition that actually goes back to Roman and Greek times.

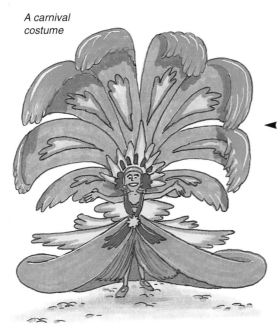
A carnival costume

Many countries hold carnivals, often at the beginning of Lent. In New Orleans, the Mardi Gras was historically of special importance to black people, for at one time this was the only day on which black slaves were allowed to celebrate.

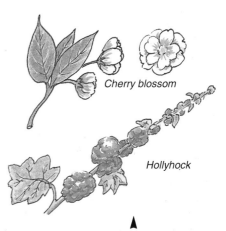
Cherry blossom

Hollyhock

Many spring festivals are held in honour of flowers. The Japanese celebrate the Hollyhock Festival and the Cherry Blossom festival. They also celebrate Setsubun to mark the change of season. To drive out evil spirits, they place beans on a shrine and later scatter them around doorways and corners of the house. Small charms are placed over the doors.

The Feast of the Passover, or Pesach, celebrates the Exodus of the Jews from captivity in Egypt. They had no time to spare as they fled across the desert, so they baked bread without leavening it. It became the custom to remember this by eating unleavened bread, or matzoh, at Pesach. At the feast the youngest child asks four questions, which are answered by the father from his readings.

Chinese lantern

The Chinese hold the Feast of Lanterns in February to mark the end of their New Year celebrations. Lanterns are lit outside most buildings and huge paper dragons are carried through the streets.

The Hindu festival of Holi takes place in March as the trees blossom. It celebrates the story of a proud king who thought he was a god. The king's son would not believe this, and so his aunt Holika wanted him to be burned to death. However, the aunt herself finished up burned to a cinder. People light a big bonfire and then on the following day they throw coloured water and powder at each other.

105

SUMMER

Most ancient peoples understood that the Sun is the main source of energy for life on Earth. Although many summer festivals celebrate historical events, most of them are concerned with worshipping the Sun.

Building work on the great stone circle of Stonehenge began in around 2200 BC. It was originally used to worship the Sun. On 21st June, the rays of the Sun break over the horizon and shine on the altar stone. Recently, the celebrations of the old religion of the Celts have been revived there.

Tish b'Av is a fast, and a sad festival, ► marking terrible events in Jewish history. In 586 BC, Solomon's temple was destroyed along with much of Jerusalem. Later, in AD 135, a Jewish hero, Bar Kochba, and his men were massacred by the Romans. In 1290, King Edward I of England banned Jews from England, beginning a process which spread across western Europe. In 1492, 150,000 Jews were driven from their homes in Spain.

Beltane was a Celtic festival held on 1st May to celebrate the beginning of summer. ► Huge bonfires were lit in an effort to encourage the Sun to shine. Cattle were driven across the last flames of the bonfires to give the animals the holy strength of the Sun. Torches were carried in processions and burning wheels were rolled downhill.

In Sweden, the 'endless' Midsummer's Day is of great importance. In ceremonies that go back to Viking times, people dance to music around gaily painted poles. They move in a clockwise direction, the direction the Sun appears to move through the sky in the northern hemisphere. Decorated ► maypoles are used in similar European traditions.

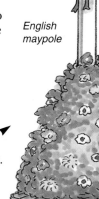

English maypole

In Japan, people celebrate Tanabata between 6th and 8th July with fireworks and paper decorations. It ► recalls the story of a cowherd and a weaver who were so much in love that they couldn't do their jobs properly. The gods separated them and placed them at either end of the Milky Way. Because they were unhappy, however, the gods allowed them to be together on this one evening.

The ancient Aztecs of Mexico honoured the supreme fire god, Xiuhtecuhtli, on 1st August. He was also known as 'He of the Yellow Face' and was important in Sun worship. His festival was called Xocotluetzi and involved the roasting-alive of slaves. However, there was ► also a jollier tradition of playing a game in which young people climbed greasy poles to win prizes.

A modern version of the baptism ceremony ▼

Whitsun is celebrated on the sixth Sunday after Easter, and celebrates the coming of the Holy Spirit to Christ's disciples. Some say 'whit' refers to the 'wit' or knowledge that made it possible for the disciples to preach in different languages. Others say it is called 'whit' because everyone who was going to be baptized was dressed in white.

Some Native American tribes celebrated the middle of summer with a four-day Sun Dance around a pole. They took no food or drink during the dance. During the Okipa ceremony, dancers pierced their chests with wooden skewers attached by ropes to the centre pole. They had to face the sun and dance without showing any pain.

In May and June, Sikhs remember the martyrdom of Guru Arjan Dev. He is seen as the apostle of peace and learning and this period celebrates the victory of good over evil. Guru Arjan Dev built the Sikh Golden Temple at Amritsar and wrote the Adi Granth, the Sikh Holy Book.

AUTUMN

Autumn is both a period of dying, as the summer ends, and a period full of life as late fruits and crops are gathered.

Diwali is the Hindu Festival of Lights held in honour of Lakshmi, goddess of fortune and wealth, the wife of Vishnu. The festival lasts for a few days in autumn and is followed by the Hindu New Year's Day. Everything is cleaned and decorated and lights are placed in the window. Debts are paid, cards are exchanged, children get gifts and plenty of food and sweets are eaten.

Ganesh Chaturthi is a celebration of Ganesha the elephant-headed son of Shiva who is the remover of obstacles. In south India it is thought by some to be unlucky to look at the Moon. One day Ganesha saw the new Moon reflected in the water and thought it was a sliver of coconut. When the Moon laughed at him, he cursed everyone who looked at it on this day.

Ganesha

Asala Perahara is a great ten-day festival held in August at Kandy in Sri Lanka. It involves a vast procession of elephants, dancers, drummer boys and torch bearers. A holy object, thought to be the Buddha's tooth, is also carried.

The Buddha's tooth

31st October, the day before All Saints' Day, is called Hallowe'en. It is the day when all the ghosts and spirits were said to be roaming about. An old Scottish prayer asks for deliverance from 'ghoulies and ghosties, and long-legged beasties, and things that go bump in the night'. Children in Britain and the United States sometimes go out to 'trick or treat'. They dress up as ghouls or witches, knock on people's doors and offer people a choice. Either they must give the children a treat or a trick will be played on them. The children also carve a face out of a pumpkin skin and light it from the inside with candles.

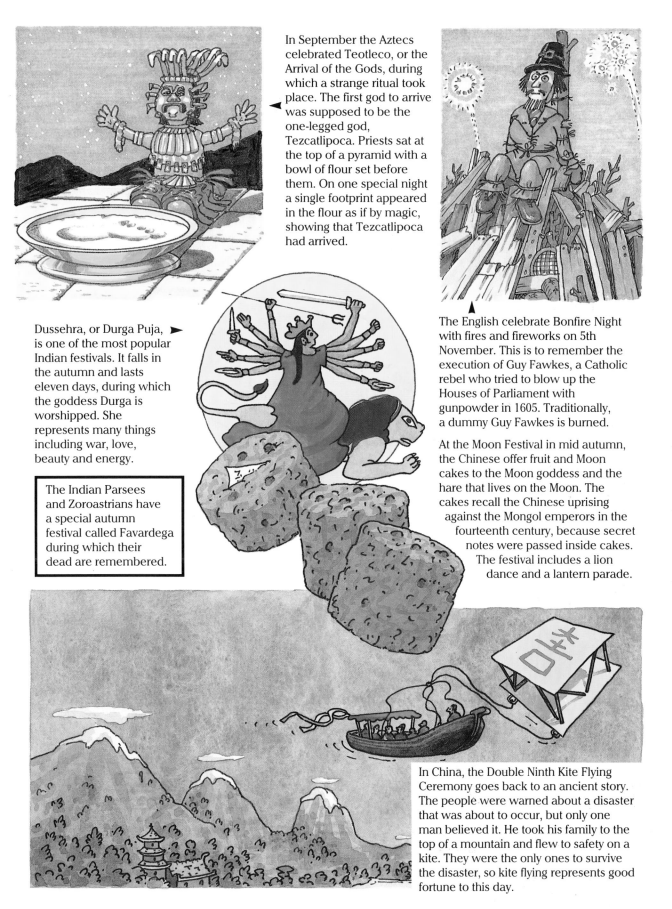

In September the Aztecs celebrated Teotleco, or the Arrival of the Gods, during which a strange ritual took place. The first god to arrive was supposed to be the one-legged god, Tezcatlipoca. Priests sat at the top of a pyramid with a bowl of flour set before them. On one special night a single footprint appeared in the flour as if by magic, showing that Tezcatlipoca had arrived.

Dussehra, or Durga Puja, is one of the most popular Indian festivals. It falls in the autumn and lasts eleven days, during which the goddess Durga is worshipped. She represents many things including war, love, beauty and energy.

The Indian Parsees and Zoroastrians have a special autumn festival called Favardega during which their dead are remembered.

The English celebrate Bonfire Night with fires and fireworks on 5th November. This is to remember the execution of Guy Fawkes, a Catholic rebel who tried to blow up the Houses of Parliament with gunpowder in 1605. Traditionally, a dummy Guy Fawkes is burned.

At the Moon Festival in mid autumn, the Chinese offer fruit and Moon cakes to the Moon goddess and the hare that lives on the Moon. The cakes recall the Chinese uprising against the Mongol emperors in the fourteenth century, because secret notes were passed inside cakes. The festival includes a lion dance and a lantern parade.

In China, the Double Ninth Kite Flying Ceremony goes back to an ancient story. The people were warned about a disaster that was about to occur, but only one man believed it. He took his family to the top of a mountain and flew to safety on a kite. They were the only ones to survive the disaster, so kite flying represents good fortune to this day.

109

Winter is the darkest and coldest season of the year. Food is often scarce in winter, though people have always enjoyed festivals of eating and drinking – perhaps to remind themselves that spring is not far away.

WINTER

Mid-winter madness

The Romans celebrated Saturnalia in honour of the god Saturn. It was supposed to be a period of chaos between the old and new year when the normal rules of society could be ignored. People drank a lot, went wild and gave presents to each other. Saturnalia was adopted by the Roman Christians and became Christmas, celebrated on 25th December.

For Christians, the most important celebration is Christmas Day, which recalls the birth of the baby Jesus in a stable in Bethlehem. Jesus was visited by shepherds and three kings who brought gifts. Most of the modern, commercial Christmas activities have little to do with Christian beliefs.

Santa Claus was originally Saint Nicholas, a Turkish bishop imprisoned by the non-Christian Roman Emperor Diocletian. Saint Nicholas was said to be kind to children and the story is told that he once brought back to life three children who had been pickled in a tub.

Father Christmas may have been based on Odin, the Norse god, who wore a long white beard and a fur-trimmed cloak. He travelled the world on his eight-legged horse Sleipnir, making sure everyone was having fun.

The Norse celebrated Yule at the time when the Sun was at its weakest. The huge Yule log was taken into the house and burned throughout the festivities. Houses were hung with evergreen plants, such as holly and ivy, as a reminder of continuing life. Today, the Swedes also celebrate the Feast of St Lucia on 13th December. A young girl is chosen and she puts a wreath with seven lighted candles on her head. She has to get up early and take food to hospitals or the houses of her friends and family.

The Jewish festival of Hanukkah takes place in December. It celebrates the defeat of Syrian-Greek invaders by Judas the Maccabee in 165 BC. The Jewish temple had been damaged by the invaders but was repaired and the menorah, an eight-branched candle, was re-lit. It is said that although there was only enough oil for one day, it stayed alight for eight. There are songs and prayers, and children play games of chance with spinning tops called dreidels.

Menorah

The Saturnalia tradition was kept alive during the Middle Ages when a winter Lord of Misrule was chosen from the peasant population. He was sometimes helped by a Queen of Misrule. They were also known as the King of the Bean and the Queen of the Pea. A pea and a bean were hidden in a cake and whoever got the slice with the pea and the bean became the King and Queen. The Lord of Misrule dressed up like a king and acted the fool, making fun of the local ruler and turning the normal social customs upside down.

The Celtic festival of Imbolc took place on 1st February. This celebrated the end of winter and a prayer for crops in the coming spring. Corn dollies from the previous crop of grain were made.

Traditional Mother Earth corn dolly

The day after Christmas is Boxing Day. It got its name from the old custom of putting money for the poor in church collection boxes. Later, tradesmen and errand boys adopted the custom and some people still give money to the milkman, postman or dustman for their service throughout the year.

Christian charity box

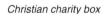

FOR THE POOR

A year is the period of time it takes for the Earth to orbit the Sun. Any day of that year could be considered the start of the following year. However New Year's Day is commonly thought of as a day in winter – though the actual date varies according to local custom or religion.

NEW YEAR

Rosh Hashanah is the Jewish New Year and occurs early in autumn. Faults and failures of the previous year are remembered solemnly. A ram's horn is blown for the service, recalling Abraham's sacrifice of a ram instead of his son Isaac.

Many people celebrate the beginning of the New Year. In Scotland, Hogmanay takes place on New Year's Eve and is an even bigger celebration than Christmas. Traditionally, people see the New Year in by joining hands and singing the song *Auld Lang Syne*. There is also a Europe-wide tradition of first-footing. Soon after New Year's Eve, someone pretending to be a tall dark stranger has to enter the house bringing a cake, a drink called 'wassail' and a piece of coal for the fire. These symbolize good luck and prosperity in the coming year.

The Celtic New Year, 1st November, was called Samhain. The priests, called Druids, gathered a plant called mistletoe which grew on the sacred oak trees. Mistletoe was cut down with a golden sickle and was used as a medicine. It was thought by some people to help women become pregnant.

At the Japanese New Year, Buddhists ring the temple bell 108 times, a sacred number, so the year will be free from evil. For those who follow the older Shinto religion in Japan, the house is decorated with evergreens (for continuing life) and bamboo (for honesty).

A torii is an ever-open gateway to each Shinto shrine

People still kiss under a sprig of mistletoe at Christmas and New Year.

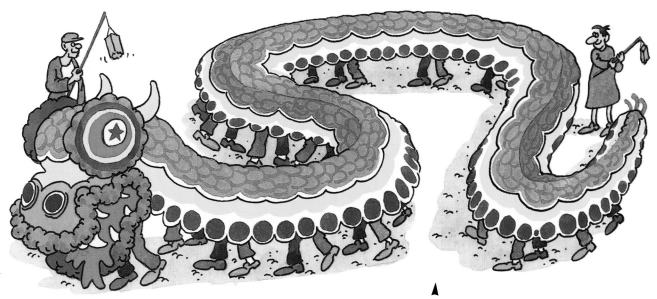

The Chinese New Year is the most important day of the Chinese calendar. In China itself, it tends to be a private celebration, but the Chinese in Britain and the United States hold big festivals in January or February. Many Chinese families keep a shrine dedicated to the Kitchen God who goes to heaven on New Year's Eve. There he reports on the family's conduct to the Jade Emperor, the god of the Taoist religion. The house is decorated with peach blossom and pictures of a carp and a fat baby, representing abundance and wealth, so that the Kitchen God will give a good report.

The day of Muharram is Islam's New Year, and commemorates the flight of Mohammed from his enemies in Mecca and his arrival in Medina. The Muslim calendar is calculated from this event which, measured on the Western calendar, occurred in AD 622.

In Japan, the New Year is marked by two festivals – the Greater and the Lesser. In the Greater Festival, prayers are offered to the dead, and friends exchange ritual gifts and visits. In the Lesser Festival, prayers for good crops are offered to the god of the rice paddy and a bird-scaring ritual takes place.

In the South Pacific region, great importance is attached to the appearance of the group of stars called the Pleiades in mid-October. This marks the end of the harvesting period and the end of the year. The festival of Makahki is held as a celebration. It is a time for feasting, sports and truce-making.

113

FARMING FESTIVALS

Late summer or autumn is the time for giving thanks for the harvest of the summer's crops. For many people it was, and still is, an important time because a poor harvest means a hungry winter.

The Michaelmas Daisy usually blooms in late September

Michaelmas (29th September) was an important day in the English farming calendar. This was the time when rents were paid and the hire of labour came to an end. It was also a time for feasting because it was at this time that farmers were paid for their crops.

In the United States, Thanksgiving Day is celebrated on the fourth Thursday in November. During the winter of 1621, half of the *Mayflower* passengers who settled in Plymouth died. The following autumn, when their harvest was a success, the colony held a Thanksgiving celebration and invited the Native Americans to join them. It was made an official holiday by Abraham Lincoln in 1863.

The Jewish feast of Shavuot in spring is a celebration of the giving of the Ten Commandments to Moses on Mt Sinai. It is also an agricultural festival when the synagogue is decorated with flowers and plants.

Sukkot falls five days after Yom Kippur and is a harvest festival. During the eight-day festival, tabernacles or booths are set up and meals, prayers and readings take place. Fruit and vegetables are hung up. Four offerings are made of a citrus fruit, palm, myrtle and willow, and seven circuits are made around the synagogue. On the last day, Simchat Torah, the year's readings of the Law are completed.

The Celtic festival of Lugnasad (1st August) was adapted and called Lammas by the Christian church. Lugnasad was a celebration of fruitfulness in which small sacrifices of food were offered to the gods. These celebrations were accompanied by sporting festivals and fairs during which marriage arrangements were made. Autumn is still a traditional time for fairs in Europe. ▲

In spring, festivals are held to celebrate the birth of farm animals and the growth of new crops. Easter in the Christian calendar was originally a pagan festival during which eggs were given as the symbol of new life. The Easter bunny comes from the hare that was the symbol of Eostre, the old goddess of spring. Eostre herself was based on the Babylonian fertility goddess Ishtar. ▼

Easter bunnies on a German greeting card

Christians in England used to celebrate the gathering of the harvest on Lammas Day. 'Lammas' comes from the Old English word 'hláfmæsse' meaning loaf-mass. Small loaves were baked from the first wheat gathered and were used in the Communion service at church. Traditionally, a corn dolly is made from the last sheaf of corn to be cut.

Following the plough

The Roman historian Tacitus described a northern European Earth goddess called Nerthus. Her temple was on a sacred island in the Baltic Sea and her priests held a spring ceremony in her honour. Nerthus's statue and her chariot were washed in a holy lake by slaves who would then have to fall into the lake and drown as human sacrifices. ▼

Later, in mainland Europe, a cart in the shape of a ship was dedicated to Nerthus. It carried a plough as a plea for fertile soil in the coming year. ▼

The January Plough Monday festival is a Christian development of pagan plough rituals. In the Middle Ages, the farm plough was decorated with ribbons. It was followed by a jester and a man dressed as a woman who was traditionally called 'Betty'. ▼

These days, where still remembered, the Plough Monday custom is for farm workers to go from house to house with a plough playing a sort of 'trick or treat'. Either householders give money to the local church or they have their doorsteps ploughed up. ▼

115

In simple farming communities, food becomes scarce during late winter and spring and it has to be carefully rationed. A period of hunger, or fasting, became part of religious custom – as did just the opposite, eating or feasting, to celebrate the availability of food. Fasting and feasting are often associated with pilgrimages, or journeys, to holy places.

Jesus spent forty days fasting in the desert before he entered Jerusalem to be crucified. This fasting before Easter is known to Christians as Lent.

FASTS, FEASTS AND PILGRIMAGES

The Sikh guru, Ram Das, ► founded the holy Indian city of Amritsar in the sixteenth century. The famous Golden Temple of Amritsar is the Sikhs' most holy place of pilgrimage.

Shrove Tuesday, or Pancake Day, is celebrated as the last day before Lent and was a chance to eat and drink well before going hungry. Pancakes were a special treat in which eggs, flour and fat that would not keep for forty days were used up. Ash Wednesday is the first day of the fast of Lent. Sinners used to scatter ash on their heads as a way of showing their sorrow. ▼

In 1445, in Olney, England, one housewife was so busy making pancakes that when the church bells rang, she ran to the church carrying the pan because she was late. The villagers of Olney now hold a pancake race every year.

Every week, Jews celebrate the Sabbath. It begins on Friday evening with a joyful service in the synagogue and then a family meal is set out with two candlesticks, a goblet of wine and two twisted loaves, a reminder of the manna, or food, that the Israelites found in the wilderness.

Yom Kippur, the Day of Atonement, follows nine days after Rosh Hashanah. Many Jews fast from sundown the day before until the sun sets. Prayers for forgiveness are offered. The blowing of the shofar, or ram's horn, signals the end of Yom Kippur.

Raksha Bandhan is a Hindu feast for brothers and sisters held in the month of Shravana (July – August). Girls tie red and gold threads around the wrists of their brothers, who promise to protect their sisters. ▶

Ramadan is a month of prayer and fasting celebrating the time when God revealed the Muslim holy book, the Koran, to Mohammad. No food or drink is taken between sunrise and sunset on each day. The fast ends with a feast called Eid ul-Fitr when new clothes are worn and cards are sent. The day is marked by acts of charity, prayers for the dead, a festive breakfast, visits and gifts for children. The festival celebrates the glory and triumph of Allah and Mohammed's work in spreading the Muslim faith. ▼

The Hajj is a pilgrimage that every Muslim is expected to make during his or her lifetime, if they can. It includes visits to the Ka'ba shrine at Mecca, to Medina and to the mountains Sinai and Ararat.

In 1858, Mary, mother of Jesus, is believed to have made eighteen appearances to a young girl, Bernadette Soubirous, in a small cave in Lourdes, France. Bernadette was declared a saint in 1933 and the cave, or grotto, has become the world's greatest place of Christian pilgrimage. Miraculous cures are said to have taken place following visits to the grotto.

117

BIRTHDAYS

In ancient societies life was often hard and survival to old age was rare. Every year of life was a triumph over death, so birthday anniversaries were joyously celebrated. Birthdays are often marked with the giving of gifts, usually to the person having the birthday. However, in some societies, gifts are offered by the one whose birthday it is.

▲

The birthday of Guru Nanak, the founder of the Sikh faith, is celebrated in November, though he may have been born in either October or April in 1469.

Elizabeth II, Queen of England, celebrates two birthdays. One is on 21st April, her birth date. She also has an official birthday on the first or second Saturday in June. This official birthday is marked by the 'Trooping of the Colour', a ceremony in which the Queen's Household Guards go on parade. This traditional ceremony was started by King George II to celebrate the birthday of his grandson (later George III), and it continued into Queen Victoria's reign. However, Victoria was usually away on holiday on her actual birthday on 24th May so she had the ceremony's dates changed to allow for an 'official birthday' celebration to be held.

In China, each year is named after one of twelve animals, and it's said that everyone born in a particular year has characteristics of that year's animal. The Year of the Rat is the beginning of the present twelve-year cycle which started on 19th February 1996. This is followed by the Years of the Ox, Tiger, Rabbit, Dragon, Snake, Horse, Goat, Monkey, Rooster, Dog and Pig. That means it will be the Year of the Rat again in the year 2008. You can work backwards to find your birth year.

The twelve Chinese years are...
▼

Monkey
(2004)

Dog
(2006)

Rat
(1996)

Pig
(2007)

Snake
(2001)

Horse
(2002)

Ram
(2003)

Rooster
(2005)

Rabbit
(1999)

Ox
(1997)

Dragon
(2000)

Tiger
(1998)

The Japanese have a Shinto birthday festival called Shichi-Go-San, which means 'seven-five-three'. All three-year-old children, as well as boys of five and girls of seven, are taken to the temple and given special sweets by the priest. Parents express their joy that their children have reached that age and pray for their wealth and happiness.

Burns' Night is celebrated by Scottish people on 25th January to commemorate the birth of the popular poet and songwriter Robert Burns. A key part of Burn's Night is the haggis. This is a sort of meaty pudding made from the innards of a cow or sheep mixed with suet and oatmeal. These ingredients are packed into the stomach lining of an animal and boiled. As it is brought into the room, bagpipes are played. Burns' poem *Ode to a Haggis* is recited before the haggis is eaten, and there is whisky drinking, music and dancing.

The Hindu festivals of Janmashtami and Ramanavami celebrate the birthdays of Krishna and Rama. These are two of the personalities of the god Vishnu.

Vishnu

Jesus Christ's birthday is celebrated on Christmas Day, 25th December. However, some modern historians say that this must be wrong because the Christmas story involves shepherds watching their flocks by night. Traditionally, shepherds in the Holy Land did not allow their sheep to gaze freely until the beginning of April.

Birth-stones

Gemstones have associations (based on saints' days and astrological signs) with each month of the year. This means that everybody's birthday falls in a particular birth-stone month.

January:
(Garnet)

February:
(Amethyst)

March:
(Bloodstone)

April:
(Diamond)

May:
(Emerald)

June:
(Agate)

July:
(Ruby)

August:
(Sardonyx)

September:
(Sapphire)

October:
(Opal)

November:
(Topaz)

December:
(Turquoise)

As well as the births and deaths of holy people, their lives or actions are also celebrated on special days.

HOLY PEOPLE

Buddhism was founded by Gautama Siddhartha, an Indian prince, in about 528 BC. He became known as the Buddha, or 'Enlightened One' after seeing a vision of truth whilst sitting under a bo tree. His teachings have been carried to many countries, especially in the Far East where the main events of his life are celebrated in May by the festival of Wesak, or Vaisakhapuja.

▼

Saints are people considered holy by the Christian church. The lives of some well-known saints are remembered on particular days, but they can't all have their own day because there are about 4,500 of them. The Christian church sets aside November 1st as All Saints' Day so that all the saints can be celebrated. Saints are often shown with a halo round their heads.

▲

Saint George is the patron saint of Portugal and England, where his day is the 23rd April. He may have been a Christian soldier who was put to death by the Romans in Palestine in AD 303. He was very popular in the Middle Ages and his flag was carried by the Crusaders in the Holy Land. There is a story about him killing a dragon and rescuing a maiden.

Patrick is the patron saint of Ireland and his day is celebrated on 17th March. He was born in England in the fourth century AD but as a teenager was carried off to Ireland as a slave. Six years later he escaped and was taken by some sailors to Gaul (France) and returned home to England much changed. He went back to Ireland to convert the people to Christianity and built a monastery at Armagh. His emblem is the shamrock, a small plant, and he is said to have driven the snakes out of Ireland.

Saint Swithin wanted to be buried outside his church rather than inside. When the monks moved his body into the church for his funeral on 15th July, AD 971, a terrible storm blew up and the rain lasted for forty days. This resulted in a saying that rain on Saint Swithin's day will be followed by forty more days of rain. ▼

Apollonia was a Christian priestess in Alexandria. When the the Romans tried to punish her for her beliefs, they broke all the teeth in her jaws. Then they built a bonfire and threatened to throw her on it unless she gave up her beliefs. Instead, she jumped into the fire and died. Her day is 9th February, and she is the patron saint of toothache. In a similar way, Saint Denys, who was beheaded, is now not only one of the the patron saints of France but also of headaches.

Ballet dancer

Saint Vitus could cure people of diseases that make people lose control of their arms and legs. One of these diseases became known as Saint Vitus's dance, so Saint Vitus was taken up by actors and dancers as their patron saint. His feast day is the 15th June.

Haile Selassie

Sikhs celebrate Baisakhi (usually on 13th April) because Guru Nanak began his missionary travels on that day.

Baha'i followers send each other cards on 29th May. This is the date in 1844 when the Baha'i founder, Ali Mohammed, declared himself the Bab, or Gate of God. A later leader, Baha'u'llah, died on this day in 1863.

Rastafarians celebrate the visit of the Emperor Haile Selassie of Ethiopia to Jamaica on 25th April, 1966. Haile Selassie ruled the only African country never to have been completely colonized by Europeans, and he is revered as the living God.

Saint Roch caught the plague and was cured when he was brought food by a friendly dog. Although unable to cure himself, Saint Roch could cure others, and so became the patron saint of plagues. His feast day is the 16th August.

121

FANTASTIC FESTIVALS

Some festivals and customs seem so strange it's often hard to understand how they started in the first place. However, now that we have them, nobody seems to want to give them up!

Every twelve years, over ten million Hindus gather on the banks of the Ganges River to share in ritual bathing at the great Kumbh Mela festival at Allahabad.

Up-Helly-Aa is a January festival held in the Shetlands. A ten-metre long Viking ship is built with a dragon's head and shields along the sides. After dark it is pulled to the seashore at the head of a torch-light procession led by a man called the Chief Guizer. Then the torches are thrown into the boat and the burning hulk is pushed out to sea.

WHO NOSE?!

Isn't Red Nose Day fun?! Every spring we get the chance to wear a silly red nose to raise money for the guys at Comic Relief. I'm glad that crazy bunch of British comedians thought it up! BUT... do you think we'll still be celebrating Red Nose Day in a hundred years' time?...

The Maori people of New Zealand used to practise cannibal sacrifices. The heart of the first member of their enemies to be killed in battle was offered to the god Tu–matavenga, the god of war. The heart, or if the person was important, the whole body, would then be eaten.

The Chinese Dragon Boat Festival has been held in early summer every year since the 3rd century BC. Qu Yuan was a poet who drowned himself in protest at bad government. It is said that a kind of dumpling made of rice wrapped in bamboo leaves was thrown into the water for the fish to eat instead of Qu Yuan. Other people splashed the water to scare away the fish. Today, long, colourful boats with dragons' heads and tails race each other with a great deal of noise and splashing to celebrate the poet. The dumplings are still made too.

Well-dressing is an ancient Celtic tradition that continues to this day in some English villages. Originally the Celts honoured the well goddesses by throwing a human skull into the well. These days wells are decorated, or dressed, in a Christian ceremony, with more pleasant objects such as flowers. It's said that no well-dressed well has ever run dry.

April Fool's Day (1st April) is a day on which people play tricks on each other. The day is associated with the time of the first cuckoo, a bird that tricks other birds by laying its eggs in their nests. A traditional joke is to send a child to the corner shop to buy 'some elbow grease' or 'a left-handed screwdriver'. Sometimes jokes are even played by newspapers or TV companies. A well respected British news programme once featured an item about the 'spaghetti tree harvest'!

The biggest celebration ever will probably take place on New Year's Eve 2000 to see in not just the new year, and the new century, but also the new millennium. However, non-mathematicians will probably celebrate the millennium a year early, on 31st December 1999!

In July, on the Feast of St Fermin, the Spaniards of Pamplona hold a dangerous and dramatic festival. Bulls are allowed to run free through the streets while men and boys risk their lives to show their skill and daring by dodging amongst them.

123

Although death is usually a sad event for the family, many religions think of death as a new beginning, either in another world, or back in this one. Sometimes the dead person is thought to be joining his or her ancestors and this is a cause for celebration.

DYING

The Parsees of India place their dead on a Tower of Silence where vultures are allowed to eat the flesh. The bones fall through a grid into a central well. Parsees believe in an event called Frashokereti when the dead of the world will be reborn and beauty and peace will reign.

The Cenotaph

The ancient Romans believed in 'Lemures', the spirits of the dead which were dangerous to the living. On 9th, 11th and 12th May it was thought that a passage opened up between the world of the living and the Underworld. The festival of Lemuria was held on these dates to ward off evil spirits. The father of a household had to wash his hands then put black beans in his mouth and walk round the house spitting them out. Ghosts were supposed to follow behind picking up the beans. No one was allowed to look at the ghosts until the ceremony had been completed nine times. The bean-spitter finally chanted, 'Shades of my fathers depart' nine times, and could then look to see if the ghosts had gone. They usually had!

Remembrance Sunday is the day on which British and Commonwealth people remember the dead of the two World Wars. On the second Saturday in November, there is a special ceremony in the Albert Hall in London with military music, prayers and a procession of veterans and flags. On the Sunday, wreaths are laid at the Cenotaph in Whitehall, in London, and services are held throughout the country. A wreath is also laid on the Tomb of the Unknown Warrior in Westminster Abbey.

The Aztecs made daily human sacrifices to the Sun god, Tonatiuh. Victims were happy to die and go to the 'Land of the Dead' because they believed that they would join an eternal, holy fire. The human sacrifices were carried to the top of a pyramid where their hearts were cut out and offered to the Sun. The dead bodies were thrown down the steps of the pyramid which would run red with blood.

When a close member of the family or a friend has died, orthodox Jews say 'Blessed be the true Judge'. They tear part of their clothes as a symbol of their grief and go into strict mourning for seven days, staying at home, wearing no shoes and sitting on a low stool. There follows a month of general mourning until a stone has been laid on the grave. ▼

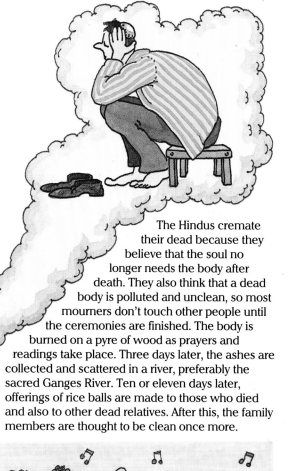

Many Chinese people believe that the dead continue to watch over their descendants from 'The Land of Shades'. They also think that the soul of someone who dies will be judged and perhaps punished. For this reason the Chinese celebrate Yu lan-p'en, when they burn specially made paper gifts such as money, houses or even cars. It's thought that these can then be taken to the next life where they may be useful to the person who has died. The body is buried with a lot of loud noises and fireworks to scare off the evil spirits. Ten years after the burial, the bones are dug up, cleaned and planted in a pot which is then buried at a new, carefully selected site. A special carved tomb is made, which the family visit during the Ch'ing Ming festival.

The Hindus cremate their dead because they believe that the soul no longer needs the body after death. They also think that a dead body is polluted and unclean, so most mourners don't touch other people until the ceremonies are finished. The body is burned on a pyre of wood as prayers and readings take place. Three days later, the ashes are collected and scattered in a river, preferably the sacred Ganges River. Ten or eleven days later, offerings of rice balls are made to those who died and also to other dead relatives. After this, the family members are thought to be clean once more.

The Sikhs believe in the re-birth of the soul and are not supposed to feel sad about death. The body of the dead person is washed and dressed and taken to the Temple. After the cremation, the ashes are scattered with flowers onto a running stream. For the following ten days the Adi Granth (the Sikh holy book) is read.

In many religions the relatives and friends of a dead person hold a wake, during which people stay up with the body to watch over it until it is buried. This was originally done to make sure the 'body' was really dead, so avoiding burying a person alive by mistake. A traditional Irish wake is a lively occasion with a great deal of drinking and feasting that can last for days.

Most countries celebrate important days and events in their history – such as a revolution or gaining independence. National holidays are usually encouraged by governments as a way of maintaining national pride. They are often marked by a day off work or school.

NATIONAL HOLIDAYS

The Swiss celebrate their Independence Day on 1st August, the date in 1291 when the Everlasting League was formed to resist the Austrian occupation of Switzerland. ▼

On 14th July 1789, French revolutionaries stormed the Bastille prison in Paris and released the prisoners. Bastille Day is celebrated on this date to mark the start of the French Revolution.

The 4th July is celebrated as Independence Day in the USA. This date marks the breaking away of the original thirteen colonies from British rule in 1776. In many towns across the country, people put on parades, barbecues, picnics, pageants and firework displays. ▼

The Peruvians celebrate their Independence Day on 9th December. This is the date in 1824 when the revolutionaries Simon Bolívar and General Antonio Jose de Sucre defeated the Spanish army at the battles of Junin and Ayacucho.

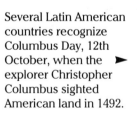

Several Latin American countries recognize Columbus Day, 12th October, when the explorer Christopher Columbus sighted American land in 1492.

The 24th October, has been set aside for all countries to celebrate United Nations Day. The United Nations is an organization set up in 1945 to try to resolve differences between nations and peoples all over the world.

United Nations flag

Colin has a problem. Some of his descriptions of ceremonies and festivals have become mixed up. Can you tell him which first lines should go with which second lines?...

COLIN'S CRAZY CALENDAR

QUIZ

1. Norsemen thought that Odin travelled the world
2. in order to win prizes.

3. On New Year's Eve, a tall dark stranger may come,
4. to stand near the fire for the next three days.

5. On April Fool's Day, a fool might try
6. riding an eight-legged horse called Sleipnir.

7. Some ancient Aztecs climbed greasy poles
8. to watch the sun rise over Stonehenge.

9. After a traditional Albanian wedding the bride had
10. the boat-burning festival of Up-Helly-Aa.

11. The patron saint of headaches is
12. bringing in a lucky lump of coal.

13. In January, Shetland Islanders may visit
14. St Denys, who had his head chopped off.

15. On June 21, Celtic priests gathered
16. to buy a left-handed screwdriver.

ANSWERS: Line 1 and line 6 (see page 110), 3 and 12 (page 112), 5 and 16 (page 123), 7 and 2 (page 107), 9 and 4 (page 102), 11 and 14 (page 121), 13 and 10 (page 122), 15 and 8 (page 106).

Index

First published in 1996 by Franklin Watts

This edition published in 2000

Franklin Watts
96 Leonard Street
London
EC2A 4XD

Franklin Watts Australia
14 Mars Road
Lane Cove
NSW 2066

© 1996 Lazy Summer Books Ltd
Illustrated by Lazy Summer Books Ltd

ISBN 0 7496 3931 8

Dewey classification: 390

A CIP catalogue record for this book is available
from the British Library.

Printed in Belgium

PRINTED IN BELGIUM BY

proost
INTERNATIONAL BOOK PRODUCTION